A HISTORY OF
LICHFIELD

Engraved by I.Greig from a Drawing by H.M.Sterndale for the Antiquarian Itinerary.

The Lichfield Willow Warwickshire.

A HISTORY OF
LICHFIELD

CHRIS UPTON

PHILLIMORE

First published in 2001 by
Phillimore & Co., an imprint of
The History Press
The Mill, Brimscombe Port,
Stroud, Gloucestershire, GL5 2QG
www.thehistorypress.co.uk

Reprinted 2011, 2012

ISBN 978 1 86077 663 2

Printed and bound in Great Britain.

Contents

List of Illustrations, vii
Introduction, xi

CHAPTER ONE	*Beside the Grey Wood*	1
CHAPTER TWO	*Lichfield New Town*	17
CHAPTER THREE	*Reforming Zeal*	33
CHAPTER FOUR	*The Bloody City of Lichfield*	49
CHAPTER FIVE	*A Society of Antiquaries*	67
CHAPTER SIX	*A City of Philosophers*	83
CHAPTER SEVEN	*Close Families*	99
CHAPTER EIGHT	*A Tale of Two Cities*	117
CHAPTER NINE	*Trains and Boats and Planes*	133
CHAPTER TEN	*Modern Times*	149

Bibliography, 167
Index, 173

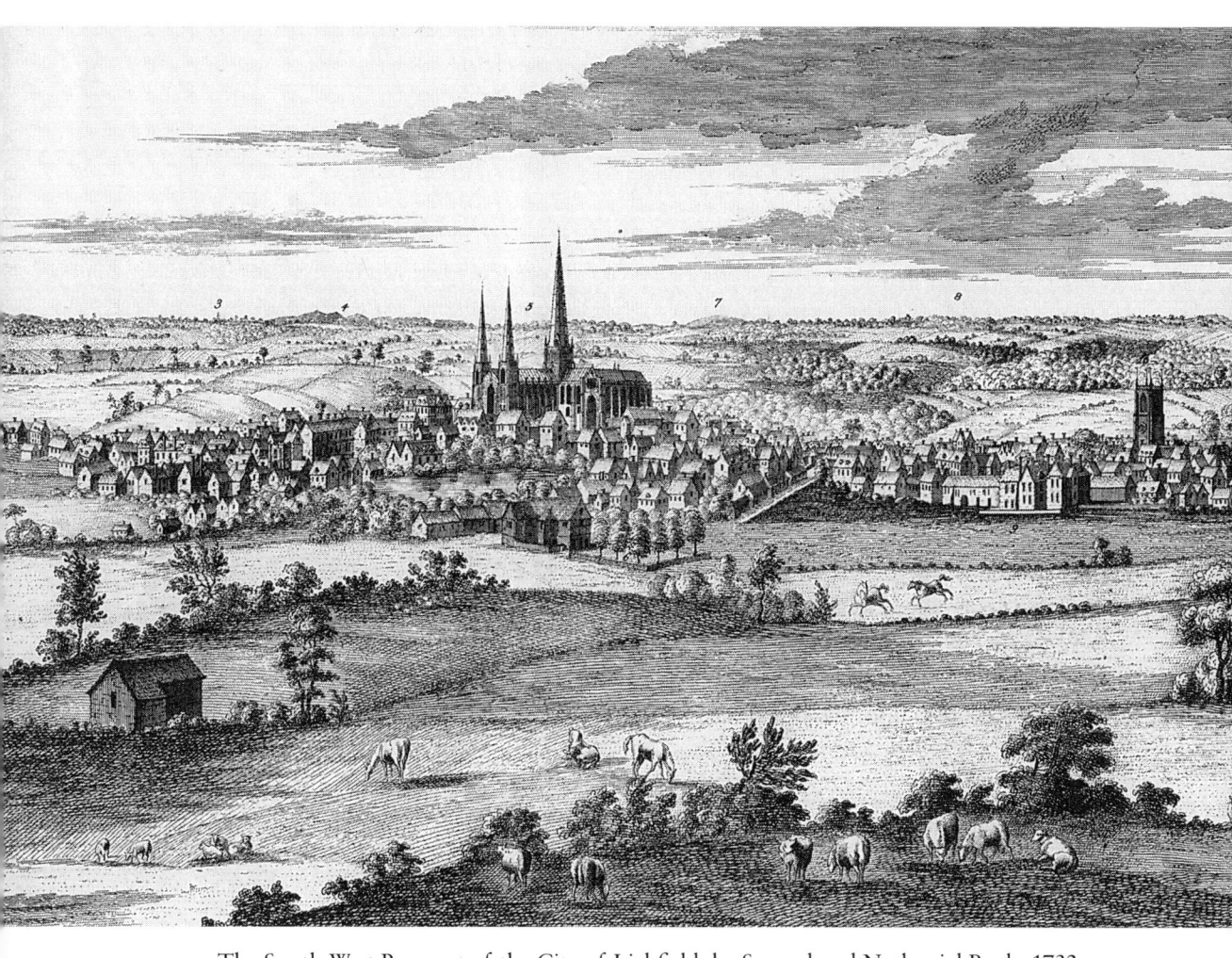

The South West Prospect of the City of Lichfield, by Samuel and Nathaniel Buck, 1732

List of Illustrations

Frontispiece: The Lichfield Willow

The South West Prospect of the City of Lichfield, by
Samuel and Nathaniel Buck, 1732, vi
1. St Mark, from the St Chad Gospels, 3
2. Interpretation of the old seal of the corporation, 4
3. St Michael's church, Greenhill, 5
4. The chapel of St Chad's Head in the cathedral, 8
5. St Chad's well, 10
6. The west end of St Chad's church, Stowe, 12
7. Old cottage and tenant near St Chad's well, 15
8. Early 18th-century prospect of Lichfield from the
south-west, 16
9. St John's Hospital, 22
10. Medieval west gate to the cathedral close, 24
11. The Crucifix Conduit, 25
12. The cathedral and Minster Pool, 1806, 26
13. The upper courtyard of the Vicars' Close, 26
14. Bore Street, c.1900, 29
15. Market Street, 1983, 31
16. Interior of the cathedral, 1813, 32
17. The gateway to the choristers' house, 34
18. The old grammar school, 1860s, 35
19. Dean Denton's market cross, 1806, 36
20. The west front of the cathedral, 1656, 40
21. What remained of the Friary complex in 1782, 43
22. Milley's Hospital, Beacon Street, 45
23. Bower cakes awaiting distribution in 1908, 46
24. The Guildhall, 1838, 48
25. Robert Greville, 2nd Lord Brooke, 54
26. The view from Prince Rupert's Mound to the north
of Gaia Lane, 59
27. Stowe Pool, 1785, 60
28. The remains of the west gate, 61
29. Major-General Sir William Brereton, 63
30. The west front of the cathedral, 1782, 64
31. Aerial view of Lichfield cathedral close, 1964, 65
32. Cathedral choir after Victorian 'improvement', 66
33. Statue of Charles II, 68
34. The cathedral without its central spire, 1646, 69
35. Elias Ashmole, 72
36. Richard Greene's museum, 1798, 75
37. Lichfield Museum, 1910, 75
38. David Garrick as King Lear, 80
39. The David Garrick theatre, Bore Street, 81
40. Charrington's, Market Street, 1952, 82

41. Statue of Dr Johnson in the market place, 83
42. Dr Johnson's birthplace, 84
43. Quoniams Lane, 86
44. Samuel Johnson painted by Joshua Reynolds, 89
45. Edial Hall, near Burntwood, 1824, 90
46. The market square, 1783, 96
47. Statue of James Boswell, 97
48. Dr Johnson's statue in the market place, 98
49. Anna Seward by Tilly Kettle, 100
50. Honora Sneyd, 103
51. Richard Lovell Edgeworth, 104
52. Stowe House, 106
53. The cathedral from the north-west, 108
54. Erasmus Darwin, 110
55. Darwin House, Beacon Street, 112
56. Thomas Day, 115
57. Lichfield union workhouse, 1843, 118
58. The entrance to the Bishop's Palace in 1953, 121
59. The Corn Exchange, 123
60. Sheriffs leaving the cathedral, 1953, 124
61. The market place, 1853, 126-7
62. Sandford Street, 1905, 128
63. The Conduit Clock, 131
64. The tomb of Thomas James Law, 132
65. The Wyrley & Essington Canal, 136
66. The railway bridge over St John Street, 138
67. City Station, c.1849, 141
68. Trent Valley Station, c.1849, 142
69. The grandstand of Whittington racecourse, 145
70. View of the city from St Michael's churchyard, 146
71. Classical portico at the corner of the Friary and Bird
Street, 147
72. Statue of Commander Edward John Smith, 148
73. Aerial view of the south of the city, 151
74. The Bower procession, 1966, 155
75. Ceremony to honour the presence of the US Army,
1944, 158
76. Bakers Lane shopping precinct, 161
77. Sir Francis Chantrey's 'Sleeping Children', 162
78. The Court of Array, 1908, 163
79. The Sheriff's Ride, 1938, 164
80. The Museum Gardens, 1955, 165
81. A Plan of the City and Close of Lichfield from Actual
Survey by John Snape, 1781, 179

Introduction

Every year on Whit Monday the city of Lichfield dusts off its history, prays for a sunny day and goes on parade. What the posters call 'Bower Day' is a distinctively English mixture of fantasy, funfair and fancy dress parade, but given decent weather there are always thousands lining the streets to watch the bower queen on her float, the brass bands and the fire brigade in their old uniforms.

The Greenhill Bower has its origins in the inspection of the watch by the bishop's steward before the Whitsun fair and as such it is documented as far back as the 15th century. Today, while the organisers are tying the last paper flower to the floats, a kind of polite parody of the original ceremony is taking place in the Guildhall. The 'court of array' has long since divested itself of any military function. Children in lycra chain-mail, carrying plastic swords, stand sporadically to attention before the admiring gaze of proud parents and assembled dignitaries. On Whit Monday 2001 I too was in the audience, a plain-clothes historian.

Arriving from Birmingham, which has long since abandoned all of its ancient traditions, and walking up to the Guildhall past the candyfloss stalls and Mr Sizzle's hot-dog stand, I could hardly find it difficult to be cynical about this quaint ceremonial survival. The antiquarian, Thomas Harwood, whose knowledge of the city exceeded most, thought as much in the early 19th century, dismissing the Bower as 'an idle and useless ceremony adapted for the amusement of children'. Anna Seward was even ruder.

But there is more to ceremony than this. What surprised me in May 2001 was that in a city of 30,000 people there was still a sense of continuity and shared purpose so rarely seen in 21st-century Britain. The local MP was busy collecting for charity, while the sheriff and mayor drove by in a car hired from a family firm of coachmakers that had operated in the city for five generations. (It now specialises in funerals.) At the court of array the dozeners no longer needed to report on the readiness of their men for defence of the realm. They could, on the other hand, take the opportunity to complain of the poor rail service, or the fouling of pavements, or of threats to the local hospital. Lichfield was alive and well.

It would be easy enough to be nostalgic in the Guildhall. Stripped of its probate and county courts, magistrates' court and quarter sessions, Lichfield's Guildhall represents the bare bones of civic power that remain after half a dozen local government reorganisations. But below the window at the south end of the hall there are paintings of the city's famous sons (and one daughter) to remind the visitor that for about 150 years – from the mid-1600s to the early 1800s – Lichfield glittered. I make no apologies for devoting three chapters to this extraordinary period. Too easily the city is simply labelled as the home of Dictionary Johnson. So it was, but it was also the cradle of Ashmole and Garrick, Darwin and Seward. It was also the home of poorer, less educated folk as well, and I hope I have done justice to them too. After all, the great and the good are always in the minority.

What Tolstoy said of families is equally true of towns. Their happiness is all the same, but their misery is individual. Lichfield has endured fewer traumas than many, but its experience of the Civil War was exceptional. In retrospect this makes for a compelling narrative, but that must not be allowed to diminish the terror and destruction it wreaked.

The sense of continuity with the past will always be palpable with Lichfield as long as the three spires – the ladies of the vale – rise above the Minster Pool. But it remains so only as long as there are people who make it their business to preserve it. My thanks are due to the dean and chapter of the cathedral, to St Mary's Heritage Centre and to the staff of Lichfield Record Office, who coped cheerfully and professionally with my many enquiries. Thanks also to Andy Willis for his draft index and scanned images, to Dave Pettit for photographs, to my wife, Fiona Tait, for enduring, just as cheerfully and professionally, my long absences at the word processor, and to my parents who continually asked whether 'it' was finished yet. I can now inform them that it is.

CHRIS UPTON

Birmingham, May 2001

CHAPTER ONE

Beside the Grey Wood

It's a historical rule of thumb that whatever the earliest evidence for human habitation you can find for a place, there will always have been something earlier. Lichfield is a case in point. For all the confidence with which we can document Lichfield's arrival on the scene in Anglo-Saxon England, there always remains the nagging suspicion that something dramatically earlier will some day emerge.

That said, the case for earlier settlements where the city of Lichfield would one day grow is not entirely a matter of guesswork. A few Mesolithic remains have been unearthed on Greenhill, in St Michael's churchyard, and evidence for Neolithic settlers has been uncovered on the sandstone ridge that forms the base of the cathedral. But after that the curtain drops, and if there were Iron-Age people in the area they were remarkably tidy, archaeologically speaking. There were, however, Iron-Age Celts not far away, for they have left something far more enduring than burials and artefacts; they have left us with a placename.

Ironically, that Celtic placename has been passed down to us by the very people who displaced them. Around AD 50 (the first secure date we can apply to the history of south Staffordshire) the 14th Legion of the Roman army arrived, intent on the conquest of the province they called Britannia. As yet, this masterplan was still in its infancy. The invasion had taken place only seven years before, and the four legions were still principally engaged in laying down the logistical infrastructure that would enable it to be achieved. For that the legions needed roads, posting stations, military camps and ideally an acquiescent native population. All four requirements were provided by the Roman base we now call Wall.

Wall is in many ways a classic example of the Roman way of doing things. The army base stood close to the junction of two Roman roads: Watling Street, heading north-west into Wales, and Ryknild Street, leading north-east towards a crossing of the Trent at Burton. A *mansio* (an early kind of coaching inn) no doubt appeared early, followed by the bath-houses and exercise yards that we associate with Roman occupation. And the magnet of soldiers with disposable income would have quickly attracted native traders to the fort. By the time Wall had served out its military purpose it would have been primarily a civilian settlement, where Celt and Roman learned to forget their cultural differences. By the 2nd century the site occupied around 30 acres.

The name 'Wall' only emerges in the 12th century, no doubt as an easy label for a place littered with Roman stonework. The Romans called it *Lectocetum* or *Letocetum*. Despite the superficial similarity between the names of the cathedral city and its Roman neighbour the connection was only recognised by a Victorian philologist, Henry Bradley, in 1886. Bradley argued for a link between the Roman placename and the (as yet) unidentified town of Luitcoit, first mentioned by the Dark-Age historian, Nennius. The native Celts in the area spoke an early form of Welsh, and in modern Welsh the name would be 'lwyd goed', translated in English as 'the grey wood'. Certainly it was not unusual for the Romans to adapt a native placename for their own purposes, as they did further along Watling Street at *Viriconium* or Wroxeter. Whether they understood the meaning of the Celtic name we do not know, but having cut their way through the extensive forests of south Staffordshire the name would not have seemed inappropriate. Those woods would later be rebranded Cannock Forest and claimed by the king, but this was still a thousand years away.

If this cocktail of Welsh and Latin still seems a long way from the name we have today, we have to wait until the 8th century for something more familiar to emerge. The Anglo-Saxon historian, Bede, refers to the place as Lyccidfelth, and so by slow linguistic steps the name becomes Licetfeld and finally Lichfield. What intrigued Henry Bradley particularly (being a student of languages) was the fact that the name 'lichfield' contained both a Celtic element – the grey wood – and an Old English or Saxon suffix, meaning 'common pasture'. Certainly it suggests that when the English first arrived in the grey wood they met a Welsh-speaking population, any residual Latin speakers having long since disappeared. But, like the Roman conquerors before them, the English adapted the native name and so fixed it upon the map of history. The pasture by the grey wood was born.

Bradley's theory, now accepted as the most plausible, provoked considerable controversy at the time, for it displaced an interpretation which had persisted for 900 years. It's worth repeating the alternative explanation, if only to show how strong social memory can be, and how politics, religion and wishful thinking can often find a common cause.

The story originates with Geoffrey of Monmouth, who attempted (in the absence of anything as useful as evidence to go on) to create an early Christian history of England. It would seem that Geoffrey single-handedly invented a Christian priest called Amphibalus, who was said to have converted St Alban and then headed off into the west to make further converts. There Amphibalus and his followers faced the full force of Roman oppression (unleashed by the pagan emperor Diocletian) and were slaughtered. The legend lay dormant for some centuries before a chronicler called William of St Albans and Matthew Paris took up the narrative. They numbered the martyrs at 999 and located the massacre at Lichfield. The word 'lich', explained Paris with some confidence, means corpse (the word 'lichgate' reflects this usage) and there-

1 *The figure of St Mark (with his symbol, the lion) from the St Chad Gospels. There is no direct connection between the saint and the gospels, but, like him, they may well have begun life in Ireland or Northumbria. The manuscript has been in Lichfield for over one thousand years, apart from a brief absence during the Civil War. Frances, Duchess of Somerset, returned it to the cathedral once peace had returned.*

fore the placename refers to a 'field of corpses', a clear reference to the massacre of the Christians. This false etymology even won over Dr Johnson.

The tale was plausible enough to inspire a host of antiquarians who followed, including John Rous, John Leland (who, to be fair, places the massacre at Caerleon), William Camden and the Warwickshire poet, John Drayton. Drayton wrote of the 999 martyrs who:

> … were slain where Lichfield is, whose name doth rightly sound
> There of those Christians slain, dead field or burying ground.

By 1345 there was even some of Amphibalus' dust preserved in Lichfield cathedral, though this seems to have blown away by the following century: Amphibalus, or so the cathedral clerics seem to have thought, was not a saint to promise much. He might easily have been expunged from the record, along with his 999 associates, had not political considerations intervened. In 1548, come the Reformation, Lichfield was incorporated as a borough, and the new civic body needed an image – what we would now call a logo – for its seal. In the divided religious atmosphere of the time it was no doubt advisable for the corporation to make a clean break with Lichfield's recent Catholic history, and to distance itself from St Chad or any figure connected with the old religion. Such was the appeal of ancient British history at the time that the corporation elected to use an illustration of the 999 Christian martyrs (or a few dismembered representatives) as its coat of arms. More curiously still and – one feels – somewhat misguidedly, the truncated bodies appeared as part of the livery of the first-class carriages of the South Staffordshire Company trains when they ran through Lichfield in the 1840s!

2 *A dramatic interpretation of the old seal of the corporation, now forming a rather gruesome rockery on the Bird Street side of the Museum Gardens. The trees presumably represent Borrowcop Hill and the spires of the cathedral can also be discerned. Lord Gower paid for the arms to be set in the front of the Guildhall in 1744.*

3 *St Michael's church at Greenhill. Much of the medieval fabric disappeared during the extensive restorations of 1842, ironically thanks to the Lichfield Society for the Encouragement of Ecclesiastical Architecture.*

To say that the new image was successful would be an understatement. The martyrs remained a potent symbol of Lichfield for the next 300 years as the appeal of the legend grew. A canon of the cathedral in the 1570s speedily identified St Michael's churchyard as the burial place of the martyrs, and the 17th-century antiquarian, Robert Plot, decided that a site in Elmhurst (appropriately called 'christianfield') had been the site of the martyrdom of the Lichfield 999 (It might have made a perfect coat of arms for the police force too.) The site was still being marked on maps in the 1920s. A stone panel showing the old coat of arms is still to be seen in the Museum Grounds in Bird Street, removed from the Guildhall during the Victorian restoration of the building. It was presumably for artistic reasons that the corporation seal reduced the 999 martyrs to just three, but this in its turn added a further variant to the story. By the 18th century the Lichfield martyrs had become three kings, presumably to match the biblical ones, and the scene of the battle was Borrowcop Hill. *Neele's Railway Reminiscences*, referring to the earliest railway excursions to the city in 1849, recalls the punctuation blunder of an early poster which advertised that:

> After viewing the Cathedral, the children will be taken to Barrow Cope Hill [*sic*], where tradition asserts the three Kings were slain for refreshment and amusement.

The tale of Amphibalus has long since been discredited, but the suggestion that there was a Christian colony in or near Lichfield before St Chad arrived in AD 669 has persisted. Two pieces of evidence have kept the belief alive, though neither of them is entirely above suspicion. Firstly a bronze bowl inscribed with the Christian Chi-Rho symbol was found at Wall in the 1930s, linking the place with the Christianised Roman Empire. Unfortunately this burial item, if that is what it was, has since disappeared, making further analysis impossible. However, given that the whole of Roman Britain theoretically converted to Christianity by order of the Emperor Constantine in AD 313, the presence of Christian symbolism would not be so unusual. It is certainly no proof that the religion survived the collapse of Roman power in the 5th century.

The other piece of evidence is even more problematic, but potentially much more interesting. It appears in the body of early Welsh poetry, in a piece of bombastic militarism known as 'The Elegy of Cynddyland', which describes an incursion by Welsh cattle raiders into England in the early 7th century. The crucial section runs as follows:

> Conflict of might, great plunder,
> Before Caer Lwytcoed did Morfael seize
> Fifteen hundred head of cattle and five litters,
> Four score steeds and trappings for mountings.
> All bishops with but one swine anywhere
> He did not spare, nor book-grasping monks.

The Welsh, it seems, had little to learn from the Vikings when it came to dealing with monasteries! The place that felt the full force of border conflict is the same one demonstrated to be the Welsh or Celtic form of Lichfield. It would be a rash historian who built theories on the shaky foundations of epic verse, but the suggestion here is that the monks and a bishop who bore the brunt of the attack were in residence some considerable time before St Chad or any of his shadowy successors. If there is any truth in the Welsh tale, then it may help to explain why Lichfield was chosen as Chad's centre of operations. But there is, it has to be said, no supporting evidence in any Anglo-Saxon literature.

Which brings us neatly onto St Chad himself. The first authentic historical figure connected with Lichfield needs little introduction. His name is attached both to the cathedral, to a number of churches in the vicinity (including Pattingham and Stafford), to the wonderful illuminated gospel in the cathedral treasury (which ironically probably has no connection with the man whatsoever) and, curiously enough, to a Victorian remand home for girls. Yet Chad's involvement with Lichfield took up only the last three years of his life, before he succumbed to plague as two of his monastic brothers had before him. However, as any medieval cleric will tell you, it's more important that a saint dies in your town than that he is born there.

Chad's origins lie in the survival of Christianity and learning in northern England and Ireland after the fall of Rome. Our most reliable source for the history of the 7th century, the Venerable Bede, tells us that Chad was sent by his father, Ceawlin, to a monastic school on Lindisfarne, along with his three brothers. If successful vocational training is the measure of a school, then Lindisfarne succeeded admirably: two of the brothers became monks, and the other two bishops. From here Chad went to Ireland, where he became a priest, and no doubt learnt the disciplines of prayer, fasting and meditation that he would later bring to Staffordshire. Once he returned to England in 653 Chad's rise up the ecclesiastical ladder was impressive, although the paganism of most of the English kingdoms at this date meant that there were not many others climbing the same ladder. After some early missionary work, Chad became abbot of Lastingham in Yorkshire, replacing his dead brother, Cedd, in that post.

Chad's subsequent career needs to be put into the context of 7th-century Christianity in Britain. Chad came from a background of Celtic Christianity, but the Synod of Whitby of 664 had effectively silenced the voice of the Celtic tradition in favour of that of Rome. It was Chad's fate to be caught up in the internal religious politics that followed from that decision. In 665, according to Bede, two men were consecrated as Bishop of York, one (Wilfrid) according to the Roman rites and another (Chad himself) following the Celtic practice. It was not simply a difference in theology, it was a difference in technique. While Wilfrid was content to stay in one place (which happened to be France), Chad lived the life of a typical Celtic bishop, living frugally

4 *The chapel of St Chad's Head in the south choir aisle of the cathedral. This was probably where the saint's head was preserved in a painted wooden box. Inside was a gilt case in the shape of a head, which could be opened to reveal the skull to pilgrims. The chapel was re-dedicated to St Chad in 1897. The head, of course, by then had long since disappeared.*

and travelling constantly around a diocese without a formally acknowledged base. But the anomaly of two bishops was not allowed to last for long. In 669 the new Archbishop of Canterbury annulled the appointment of Chad to York and transferred him instead to Mercia. This, at least, was a permanent appointment, if only for the remaining three years of the saint's life.

The vast diocese which Chad was asked to administer was just as problematic as the ecclesiastical politics that had driven him there. Mercia was ostensibly an independent kingdom, though for much of the century it lay under the shadow of the more powerful kingdom of Northumbria. The marriage of Peada of Mercia to the daughter of King Oswiu of Northumbria in 653 gave the Mercian king some measure of protection (the leaders of the two kingdoms had a terrible habit of killing each other), but only if Peada, like his Northumbrian overlord and his wife-to-be, converted to Christianity. From this point onward Mercia had a bishop, but to a man they all came from the north. According to Bede the first two office-holders were actually Scotsmen.

Quite how much we trust in the names or even the existence of these first bishops (Diuma and Ceollach, Trumhere and Jaruman) depends on how much we trust Bede himself, but even if we do so, there is nothing to link them specifically with Lichfield. As has already been said, Celtic bishops tended to be peripatetic, though they no doubt were found temporary rest in a monastery somewhere. Only with Chad do we see the Mercian diocese linked to what was to be its new centre. The decision was unlikely to have been Chad's alone; the opinions of the new king, Wulfhere, no doubt carried considerable weight. Anglo-Saxon kings were also peripatetic, but that does not preclude them having a main base; it may have been at Tamworth (as it was later) or at Bury Bank near Stone. Neither place was far from Lichfield. Nearer still, it seems that Borrowcop Hill, to the south of the city, was also an Anglo-Saxon burh or fortification, although its exact purpose or date is unknown. Certainly its earlier name – Burghwaycop – suggests so, distantly recalled in the 'castle ditch' that skirted it in the 13th century. Whatever Saxon fort had once stood there, it was subsequently replaced by a sheep fold, and later still by what they called a 'temple' in the 17th century and we would call a folly.

Whatever the reason for the decision, Bede tells us that Chad chose Lichfield as the centre of his episcopal see, and describes something of the new bishop's life there:

> He had built himself a dwelling not far from the church, where he was
> accustomed to pray and read with seven or eight of the brethren, as often
> as he had any spare time from the labour and ministry of the word.

The location of the church and the dwelling have never been conclusively established. It seems likely that the former was on or near to the site of the cathedral and was probably a wooden structure. Bede calls it St Mary's. As for Chad's place of retirement, this may well have been at Stowe. It was, after all, only a ten-minute stroll for a man who was used to walking a great deal further. Certainly Stowe's association with Chad was strong by the 12th century, when there was a church there dedicated to him. The aura of Stowe as a place of spiritual contemplation (the name itself means 'holy place') was reinforced by the presence of a holy hermit or anchoret during the 1400s. The bishop supplied him with firewood and he lived in a small cottage in the churchyard.

5   *St Chad's well with its most recent roof. Writing in the 1680s, Robert Plot remarks that 'They have a custom in this county of adorning their wells on Holy Thursday with boughs and flowers ... diverting themselves with cakes and ale, and a little music and dancing ...'.*

As for the holy well near the church, where St Chad was reputed to have prayed naked, this too had become a popular tourist attraction by the 16th century, when the antiquarian, John Leland, visited it. Veneration of wells (surely of a tradition of pagan origin) is common in Staffordshire and Derbyshire, but the established church, whether Catholic or Anglican, has never been entirely comfortable with the idea. Certainly the well was in a sorry state by the beginning of the 19th century, when antiquarian interest in it began to revive. In the 1830s James Rawson, a local physician, saw to it that the water supply was improved and an octagonal stone structure was erected, a feature that lasted until another renovation in the 1950s. (In the meantime the mystical spring was found to need a pump to coax it to the surface.)

The well remained a favourite place of pilgrimage and veneration throughout the 20th century both for Anglicans and Catholics, but the popularity that the church at Stowe attracted at the end of 2000 was both unexpected and bizarre. It came courtesy of the global information system known as the Internet and of the American presidential election. In the aftermath of the disputed election result in Florida, the word 'chad' gained sudden notoriety, not as the name of a long-dead saint, or even of a comic character beloved by graffiti artists, but as the term for the dimple punched into ballot cards by Florida's mechanised voting machines. As countless millions logged onto their computers to find out more about Florida and its chads, the world-wide-web directed them effortlessly to the web site of a small church in Staffordshire. No ecclesiastical home page has ever excited such interest.

Chad lived less than three years in Lichfield, dying of the plague on 2 March 672, but his influence in death was probably far greater than in life. According to Bede, Chad's body was buried near St Mary's church and then transferred (in 700) to a new church, dedicated to St Peter, which we presume was built specifically to house the remains. It did not take long for the shrine to become a place of pilgrimage and (inevitably) of miracles. Bede's description of the site illustrates how blurred was the line between miracle and magic:

> The place of the sepulchre is a wooden monument, made like a little house, covered, with a hole in the wall, through which those that go there for devotion usually put in their hand and take out some of the dust, which they put into water and give to sick cattle or men to drink, upon which they are presently eased of their infirmity and restored to health.

The fledgling new diocese and cathedral needed Chad as much in death as in life, and though the saint never achieved the popularity of a Becket or a Cuthbert, the successive rebuildings of the shrine and the chapel that held it show the importance that was attached to the saint's remains. Important enough, it seems, for at least one and perhaps more of the kings of Mercia to choose to be buried near them.

Early in the 14th century Bishop Langton ordered the construction of a new shrine in Paris at a cost of £2,000, whilst other church officials gave gold and silver vessels to adorn the altar. It must have been shortly after this that the bones of Lichfield's saint began a quite extraordinary migration, a journey which would only end (unlikely as this seems) in Victorian Birmingham.

Sometime in the 14th century (we assume) the cathedral officials made the hard-nosed decision to divide up the saint's remains, probably to allow easier access to them by pilgrims. A curious notion, this, but not a problem for the medieval church, which believed that the general resurrection of the dead at the Last Judgement would reassemble the parts anyway. An inventory of the cathedral's holiest relics, drawn up by a sacrist in 1345, indicates that by this date St Chad's head was in a painted wooden case, one arm was in a reliquary, a few other bones were in a portable shrine and the rest lay in the main shrine that Bishop Langton had constructed behind the main altar. The cathedral also boasted, incidentally, some bones of St Laurence, and various bits of Golgotha and Mount Calvary.

But it was with the Reformation that Chad's really big adventure begins, almost 900 years after his death. A dead saint was something of a liability once Henry VIII began stripping the monasteries, and certainly the reliquaries and

6 *The west end of St Chad's church at Stowe, photographed in 1952. The large size of the church for such a small village reflects its importance as a Christian centre and a place of pilgrimage from Norman times onwards. There was both a cricket and a football team attached to St Chad's in the 1880s, but any player using bad language during a match was expelled!*

statues were swiftly despatched in 1538. To pre-empt the destruction of the relics themselves, a prebendary of the cathedral called Arthur Dudley spirited the bones away, taking them to a family home near Dudley for safekeeping. From here they passed to two Catholic brothers in Sedgley, who divided the relics between them. In the turbulent days under the Tudors the bones were hot property, and they remained hidden for most of the next century. We next hear of them in 1650s, when the Jesuits tracked them down. By then they may have been in Wolverhampton.

It has to be said that the progress of these venerated remains between the cupboards of various Catholic families in the Midlands remains a mysterious one even to this day. Rediscovery by the Jesuits was itself no protection, since they too were outlaws. The house of one was broken into by soldiers in 1658 and the bones dispersed once more. Sub-divided yet again, the Jesuits took some of the bones to Flanders and by 1671 they were in Liège. What remained in England were re-boxed by Father William Atkins and moved to a safer location.

The next guardians of the relics seem to have been the Fitzherbert family of Swynnerton Hall in Staffordshire. Their reappearance in 1837 could not have been better timed, and indeed the timing seems almost too good to be true. With the new Catholic cathedral in Birmingham about to open its doors, the rediscovery of the relics and their removal to the new church gave it a link with the past its builders could hardly have anticipated. According to the story a key was found at Swynnerton with a note attached, explaining that the key fitted the chest containing the remains of St Chad, which had migrated with the Fitzherberts to Aston Hall in Shropshire. And there, as promised, the box did indeed lie beneath an altar in the chapel.

Having examined the contents of the Aston chest the catholic bishops, Walsh and Wiseman, declared them (surely more in hope than expectation) to be genuine, and in 1841 they made their final move to the newly consecrated Cathedral of St Chad in Birmingham. And here, breathless after all those centuries of rushing around, they have remained ever since.

It hardly seems credible, after 500 years of division and dispersal, that the bones unearthed in 1837 could bear any relation to the 7th-century saint. The proof of the pudding, then, was scientific testing, and in 1996 the bones were despatched to the Oxford Radiocarbon Accelerator Unit for accurate dating. The results of those tests were as surprising to the investigators as they were welcome to Birmingham's Catholic community. The bones tested at Oxford consisted of one right tibia, two left tibia, a right femur and two left femora. Clearly these could not have all come from the same individual, and indeed may have belonged to as many as five. Carbon dating, however, did confirm that all the bones were from the 7th century. The physical remains of St Chad in Birmingham may now have company, but at least he has companions of his own age.

At the time of Chad's death the diocese of Lichfield was coterminous with the kingdom of Mercia, a huge tract of territory stretching from the Humber to the Thames and the Severn. That the ecclesiastical heart of this vast realm was a small church, without as much as a village to service it, was hardly ideal, and soon after 672 Archbishop Theodore set about reorganising the diocesan structure in central England. Separate dioceses were carved out of the old one, centred at Leicester, Worcester, Hereford and (we believe) Dorchester. Lichfield, however, retained its prime importance, both as the burial ground of Mercian kings and as a place of pilgrimage. There may also have been a writing-school attached to the cathedral, akin to those centres of learning in Northumbria and Ireland. Sadly, if this is the case, it has left us nothing to appreciate in the way of illuminated manuscripts or literary works. Even the superb illuminated text known as the St Chad's Gospels, still displayed in the cathedral, was not a local production. Most likely it comes from the north or the west, only finding its way to Lichfield (via Wales) in the 10th century.

But if Lichfield felt somewhat stripped of power at the end of the 7th century, the century that followed provided more than enough compensation. Under King Offa (757-796) the status of Mercia grew considerably in the hands of a man who was rather more than a regional king. Such was his authority, and the inextricable link between temporal and spiritual power, that the ecclesiastical balance tilted in favour of the Midlands. In 787 at the Council of Chelsea Offa stripped Canterbury of part of its province and gave it to Lichfield, thereby creating a third archbishopric in England, a decision confirmed by the pope in the following year. Thus Hygeberht, the current incumbent, instantly became Archbishop of Lichfield, and in that role buried King Ethelbert of East Anglia (whom Offa had executed) in his cathedral. But no doubt Hygeberht was realistic enough to recognise that his newly exalted position ultimately depended upon the heartbeat of Offa, and when that stopped in 796 the archbishopric effectively went with him. Although he clung onto it until the end of the century, the archbishopric was abolished in 803, never to return. It was, in a sense, the last flowering of Lichfield in the Saxon age. The years to come were far less secure.

We know little of the fate of Lichfield in the times that followed, but all the indications are that they were rough. The River Trent which had brought Romans to the Midlands washed up new invaders in the shape of Vikings, and there were rich pickings to be had in Lichfield's churches. Nor is there any evidence that Lichfield was fortified against such attacks as Tamworth was. Worse still, the deal struck between King Alfred of Wessex and the Scandinavian leader, Guthrum, in the 880s left Lichfield in the cold, consigned to the unofficial Viking kingdom known as the Danelaw. It's surely wrong to characterise every Viking as a pillager of monasteries, but at the very least the cathedral and diocese of Lichfield lay neglected and poorly financed.

7 *An old cottage and its tenant near St Chad's well. If poverty and spirituality are close companions, then Stowe accommodated them both. A row of cottages near the church called Littleworth was maintained as poorhouses in the 18th century. The cottages were replaced in the 1940s by a single dwelling for the caretaker of the well.*

Mercian scholars doubtless recognised which side of the border their bread was buttered, and joined the brain-drain from falling Mercia to rising Wessex.

All the evidence from this period suggests a place in temporary, if not terminal, decline. By the time of Domesday Book the number of canons at the cathedral had dropped from 20 to five, and there may have been a period without a bishop at all. When local government was reorganised into shires Lichfield missed out here too. While comparable places such as Worcester and Hereford became county towns, in Staffordshire the focus shifted to Stafford. From that point onwards Staffordshire became the most decentralised county in England, its economic, political and ecclesiastical centres remaining many miles apart.

Worse still was to follow for Lichfield. Having been stripped of its political significance, it was shortly to lose its bishop as well. The story is a complex and not especially edifying one of ecclesiastical *realpolitik*, so let us summarise it briefly. Again it was the lack of an urban centre to support its ecclesiastical

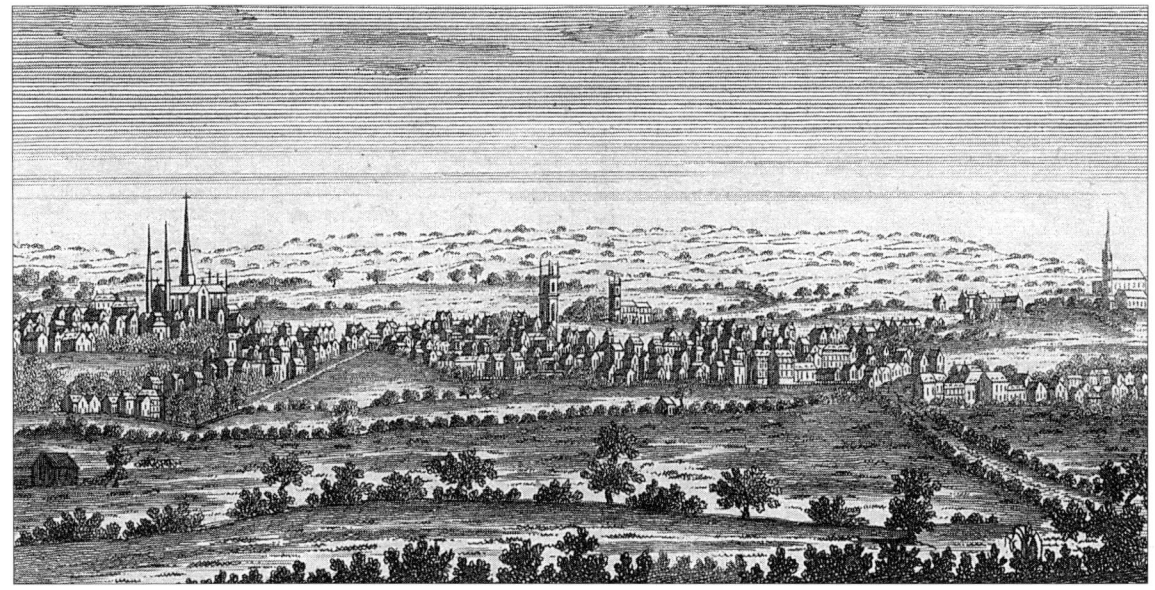

8 *An early 18th-century prospect of Lichfield from the south-west, showing its four ancient churches. Even at this date the city was a string of settlements rather than a unified entity. The medieval bank and ditch, outlined by trees, can still be seen, distinguishing the town from its rural surroundings.*

status which did not help Lichfield's cause. It had long been church policy (though not always enforced) that sees should be located in large towns and in 1075 Archbishop Lanfranc gave permission for the see to be moved to the growing town of Chester. The move may not have happened if the first Norman bishop of Lichfield had not had designs on expanding his empire westwards into Wales, but in this he was singularly unsuccessful. A generation later (in 1102) the see had been moved once more, this time to Coventry. The latter could claim with more justification to be a major urban centre, probably the fourth largest in England, though the importance of the priory there was probably of more significance. The upshot of all this was that for the next 500 years there would be a Bishop of Coventry and Lichfield, with a *cathedra*, or bishop's seat, located both in the priory cathedral of Coventry and in the older cathedral of Lichfield. The arrangement was unique in England, but was hardly a happy one, encouraging the worst sort of clerical in-fighting. But more of that anon. In the meantime it was clear that Lichfield could only recapture its former glory if it had a new town to go with its old church.

CHAPTER TWO

Lichfield New Town

We can usually rely on William the Conqueror's commissioners to throw early light on the development of an area. Our excitement at their arrival would no doubt be matched by the hostility accorded at the time to any approaching taxman. What the assessors found in Lichfield in 1086 was a collection of small settlements scattered across the landscape, hardly anything that could be called a town. Little that Domesday Book says helps us to imagine what the place was like in this period of transition from Anglo-Saxon to Norman. Much topographical work has therefore been undertaken (using later maps, the measurement of building plots and apparent deviations in road patterns) in an attempt to uncover what urban or pre-urban settlements lie beneath Lichfield's subsequent development, but it has to be said that this is far from conclusive. There may have been one settlement around Beacon Street and Gaia Lane, north and west of the cathedral, as there certainly was by the next century, another at Stowe, and perhaps a third at Greenhill near St Michael's church. At its most optimistic the evidence also suggests a row of houses to the south of Stowe Pool, along what were to become Stowe Street and Lombard Street.

Woodland and water would certainly have attracted the attention of the Domesday commissioners, for they had commercial (and therefore taxable) value, and Lichfield had plenty of both. The artificial pools which still divide the cathedral close from the town were already present, as they no doubt had been in Chad's time. The pools would have provided fish (much needed by the canons), but would also have driven water mills for the grinding of corn and malt. Domesday Book refers to two mills in the principal estate of the bishop and it seems likely that these stood where later medieval mills turned: one by St Chad's church at Stowe and the other on Dam Street, later referred to as Castle Mill or Malt Mill. All Lichfield's brewers and bakers were obliged to take their corn and malt to the bishop's mills for grinding and no doubt others did so as well. It's hard to appreciate just how vital mills were to the local economy until you look at contemporary accounts. In 1298, for example, the two mills were valued at £33 6s. 8d., considerably more than the rest of the town put together. But the costs of repair and maintenance were also high. In 1312-13 the huge sum of £78 was spent on the two mills, including the transport from Derby of two new millstones for Castle Mill.

Stowe Pool and Minster Pool (it is helpfully referred to as 'the Bishop's Fish Pool' in the Middle Ages) were, however, something of an obstacle to easy access to the cathedral close. Swimming might have been an appropriate act of penance for a pilgrim to St Chad's shrine, but it was not ideal. There were, therefore, two crossing-points: one by ferry across Minster Pool and the other via a causeway now preserved as Dam Street, and one might well imagine homesteads lining these two routes to the water. Curiously the dean and chapter of the cathedral continued to pay a fee to the corporation for a landing-stage long after the ferry had ceased to be used.

What is clear from a cursory reading of Domesday Book (not a document, it has to be admitted, that responds well to cursory reading) is the power and wealth of the bishop, whether at the time he was calling himself Bishop of Lichfield, Coventry, Chester or a combination of all three. By 1086 he already held estates in five counties, both rural manors and burgages in towns, and these holdings would increase considerably over the next couple of centuries. To his 12 manors in Staffordshire came a further 1,500 acres in Cannock Forest and around Lichfield, granted by Henry II in 1155. Henry may not have been on good terms with the 'turbulent priest' at Canterbury, but he seemed to get on famously with the bishop of Lichfield. So too his successor, Richard I, who sold off more Staffordshire manors to Bishop Nonant to fund his crusading. By the end of the 13th century, when the bishop's estates finally stopped growing, he also owned mineral workings – iron and coal – around Cannock and Rugeley, as well as a stone quarry. With this land, fortified by royal charters, came all the paraphernalia of feudal overlordship – sac and soc, waif and wreck, view of frankpledge, infangentheof, common fines and market tolls – all of which contributed significantly to the episcopal coffers.

Yet in spite of all this Lichfield was one of the poorest of the medieval dioceses (only Rochester and Chichester were assessed as worth less in 1535), and its relative poverty deterred more than one ambitious cleric from accepting the post as bishop. Certainly his overheads were not small. There were, of course, the palaces to maintain and staff, and the bishop of a diocese as large as this had several. In 1448, to balance his books, Bishop Booth demolished a number of residences, leaving himself only with homes in Coventry (which he rented out), Lichfield, Eccleshall, Hayward, Beaudesert and a town house on the Strand in London. In addition, the wages of officials – bailiffs, keepers and stewards – took up almost 15 per cent of the income from his temporalities. He must sometimes have wondered where the next haunch of venison was coming from.

The question of exactly who was to be the bishop was even more complicated than that of managing the finances. The idea of a joint diocese of Lichfield and Coventry had always been a recipe for disaster, and so it was to prove. Coventry (a monastic priory) and Lichfield (a secular foundation of dean and canons) were radically disparate institutions and such differences came to the fore at the time of appointment of a new bishop. Whatever rights (exclusive or not) the canons of Lichfield claimed for themselves in electing a bishop, they did not go down well in Warwickshire and, if that was not disruptive enough, the king, the archbishop and the pope might want a say as well. In 1215 Bishop Durdent was enthroned (and presumably elected) in Coventry, only to find the doors of his other cathedral stoutly barred against him, whilst in 1224 the dispute over the election found its way to court (and then to Rome), where it dragged on for four years. These arguments were only truly settled when the choice was taken out of the hands of canons and monks alike in the mid-14th century. From then on the tug-of-war was solely between the king and the Vatican.

The decision of who was to be bishop was a crucial one for Lichfield, for his secular power was as great, if not greater, than his religious authority. No more clearly is this shown than with Bishop Roger de Clinton, who was elected to that office in 1129. If St Chad is the first major figure to be associated with the city, then Roger de Clinton is his obvious successor. The contrast between the two could hardly be greater: between the reclusive saint and the worldly bishop. But Bishop Clinton faced and dealt with the problem that Chad had bequeathed to him – how to make an isolated settlement like Lichfield of sufficient stature to support and justify a cathedral. The issue was a pressing one. Not only was the bishop's purse suffering from a lack of income, but the rural nature of the settlement had led directly to the removal of the bishop's seat to Chester and then to Coventry. William of

Malmesbury's contemporary description of the place (to justify that decision) underlined the point:

> Lichfield is a tiny village in Staffordshire, far from the busy life of towns, in the midst of a wooded district. A stream of water flows through it. The church was on a cramped site revealing the mediocrity and abstinence of men of old, a place unworthy of the dignity of a bishop.

But by the time that William wrote these lines, remarkable changes were afoot in that 'tiny village'. For one thing the old Anglo-Saxon cathedral had been pulled down and replaced by a new building in the Romanesque style. This work had begun some years before Bishop Clinton ascended the chair, but he probably completed it, and fortified the surrounding close. However, it was south of the close that the most important changes were taking place: Roger de Clinton was creating a new town.

The idea of a new town is something we tend to associate with post-war planning, but it was as much a reality in the early Middle Ages, though it is a fact that has only been recognised in recent times. Yet one only needs to look at a map of Lichfield (whether that map is a modern or an ancient one) to see that the central area was no haphazard creation. A series of parallel streets were created, forming as it were the rungs of a ladder between the important thoroughfares of St John Street/Bird Street on the western side and Tamworth Street/Dam Street on the east. Those called Market Street, Bore Street, Wade Street and Frog Lane still survive, and the presence of a fifth is suggested by the alignment of Cock Alley and Quoniams Lane. There may have been a sixth to the north of this as well. Even the breadth of the streets was a matter of careful consideration. Three were 40 feet wide, while the fourth – Bore Street – was clearly designated as the main street of the new town by being twice that width and leading directly to what was to be the market place in the north-east corner of the town. The name of the street was originally Bord Street, perhaps alluding to the boards on which market produce was laid. Having laid down the grid of streets, it was now a matter of populating them.

The layout of streets was only one part of a large financial equation. The overall aim, after all, was to increase the value of the manor for its lord, and that was to be achieved by the creation of a market, which would in turn attract traders and manufacturers to settle there. Within the new grid the land was subdivided into burgage plots, each having an annual fixed rent of

12d. The size of these original plots is uncertain, because of later subdivision, but it was common in other new towns for burgage plots to be 40 feet wide and 80 feet deep. The charter for a weekly Sunday market is dated 1153, under Bishop Durdent, but it may have been functioning earlier, as was often the case. The circular argument that a town depended upon a market, and a market upon a town, is not easy to straighten historically. What is certain is that Lichfield was the first town in Staffordshire to receive a market charter, 70 years before Walsall and over 100 years before Wolverhampton. As such it benefited enormously from being first on the scene and from changes in the road patterns of the area. The old Roman road that had once taken transport and commerce past Lichfield had been abandoned in favour of what we now call the A51 and the A34. Both Lichfield and Newcastle to the north were now on the main drag from London to Chester, and it can hardly have been simply fortuitous that there were new towns and new markets to take advantage of the fact.

But the establishment of any borough was not complete until it was effectively defended, and so a bank and ditch were cut (considerably cheaper than a wall) from a point on Stowe Pool in a semi-circle to St John Street (beside the Hospital) and a little beyond. Gates too were added: Beacon Street gate, Colstubbe gate at the approach from St John Street (the road was earlier known as Colstubbe Street); Tamworth gate where the ditch met Tamworth Street; and Stowe gate at the top of Lombard Street. The northern approaches to the town were already sufficiently guarded by the cathedral close and by the pools. In addition, the enclosing of the town allowed tolls to be levied more effectively, as well as giving the new burgage-holders that all-important sense of privileged access.

The erection of Colstubbe gate explains the position of St John's Hospital some distance from the town centre. The hospital represents one of Lichfield's most important medieval survivals and an early introduction to the city's heritage for any tourist who arrives by train. It was reputedly founded by Bishop Clinton (though there is no certainty of this) for a prior and religious community of brothers and sisters, along with lay brethren and servants. The name 'hospital' does not, of course, mean that health care was its primary aim. It was, in a sense, both almshouse and guesthouse, providing long-term or temporary accommodation for the poor and for travellers, no doubt on their way to St Chad's shrine. Its situation at least compensated the pilgrim for arriving after the gate was closed at night. (The gates to the cathedral

9 *An engraving of St John's Hospital from Stebbing Shaw's* Antiquities of Staffordshire *(1798). In 1786 each of the almsmen received 2s. 6d. a week for maintenance, 10s. 6d. a year for coal and 1s. a year pocket money. He also received a new gown from the master every four years. Prayers for Bishops Clinton and Smith were said every morning in the chapel (except on Fridays), a tradition which still continues.*

close were also locked between eight or nine in the evening and seven in the morning.)

The chapel (rebuilt, at the time of a general re-foundation of the hospital by Bishop William Smith in 1495-6) was a place of worship for the residents, but was also needed for the singing of obits and masses for the souls of those who left gifts to the institution, of whom there were many. They included, for example, William Young, a Lichfield goldsmith, who in the late 1300s gave a burgage and a half, as well as other land and rentals, in return for a daily mass to be sung by one of the brethren. However, any impression of St John's spiritual purity is rather dispelled by the evidence from the bishop's visitations in 1331 and 1339. The brethren were clearly not living up to their vows of chastity and obedience, though the fact that the rules of the house were not being read out might explain their ignorance of them. There were accusations of inappropriate spending and of begging in the street, and the behaviour of one brother, Hugh of Wychnor, was so bad that he was confined to his chamber on a diet of bread and water. A little earlier, the dean's court had been dealing with another brother, Richard del Hull, on a number of charges of assault, mostly in church. The deposition stated that 'he does not wear his habit, but goes about as a renegade. He is a common tradesman and a trouble-maker.' Richard's brush with canon law did not unduly ruin his career: he became prior of St John's in 1330. Nor did the accusations undermine the long-term health of the hospital; the statutes drawn up by Bishop Smith in 1495 were still regulating the community well into the 20th century.

Similarly long-lived has been the hospital on Beacon Street, founded by Bishop Heyworth in 1424. Its name, Dr Milley's Hospital, commemorates the canon who re-founded the institution in 1502, and who specified that the residents should be 15 poor women. Although the number of almswomen supported by the endowment has now dropped to eight, the hospital still survives, and still occupies the site set aside for it almost 600 years ago. It is the good fortune of cathedral cities (and the folk who dwell there) to be well endowed with almshouses.

St John's Hospital was not the only religious house founded in the 13th century. By 1237 the Franciscan Friars were building to the west of the city, on a site now crossed by The Friary. The land was given them rent free by the bishop, as was the timber, supplied from the royal forests. (Who supplied them with their tennis court, which stood in the grounds, is not known.) It is not easy to judge the size or the wealth of the community, but it was not insignificant. Across the country the Grey Friars (obliged to beg for their upkeep) attracted considerable gifts and bequests and Lichfield was no exception. The fire that burnt down the friary in 1291 only enhanced their reputation as 'the deserving poor'. Even their water supply came with no strings attached. In 1310 Henry Bellfounder (a name inherited from the trade of his father) gave the friars free access to his springs at Fowlewell (we hope that the quality of the water did not reflect the name of the source) near Aldershawe, about half a mile away. They were allowed to pipe it to the friary and to erect a stone conduit, as long as they did not give even a small cup away without the donor's express permission.

Henry's generous gift reflects the importance of a pure and reliable water supply to a town with limited access to wells. The cathedral and close were early beneficiaries of this. Water was being piped from springs at Pipe (hence, presumably, its name) at Burntwood from the 1100s, a source that was still flowing 600 years later. It was also a source of considerable controversy. In

10__*The medieval west gate to the cathedral close from Thomas Harwood's* Antiquities of the Church and City of Lichfield *(1806). The gate was demolished in 1800 when Newton's College was built. The college was, in fact, yet another almshouse, this time for the widows and unmarried daughters of the clergy, and was endowed with £20,000 by Andrew Newton, the son of a Lichfield brandy merchant. A combination of war, philanthropy and road-widening has destroyed all signs of Lichfield's medieval gates.*

the 1290s the canons were in dispute with Thomas of Abnall over access to the pipes that crossed his land, and in 1489 the canons had to petition the king, when the lord of Pipe (and his wife) smashed the aqueduct and conduit. As for the town, it tapped into the supply from the close, and the aqueduct that ran from there to the market gave Conduit Street its name. There was also a conduit outside the friary (despite what Henry Bellfounder had stipulated) and women also regularly entered the cathedral close to fill buckets from the conduit there, their behaviour (or perhaps the temptations put in the canons' way) causing something of a scandal in 1516. The conduit in the close, incidentally, was known as 'Moses', a witty reminder of the miracle that the prophet performed in the desert with his trusty staff. It should be added that none in Lichfield, with the exception of the canons, and one or two other lucky individuals, had water in their houses; water was something you had to go shopping for.

We cannot pass over these many references to conduits without mentioning perhaps the most famous of all. It was in 1545 that Hector Beane, the master of the guild of St Mary and St John, set aside the guild lands in Cannock and Norton Canes, the income from which was to maintain and improve Lichfield's pipes and aqueducts. The Conduit Lands Trust was a remarkably foresighted move to guarantee that this vital supply did not suffer from the ugly wranglings of earlier centuries, and it did so well into the 1900s. Admittedly the Trust was in the habit of lavishing quite large sums on gilding, painting and decorating the conduits, but neither money nor water were in short supply. The growing wealth of the Trust also allowed it to make considerable contributions to many other aspects of civic life, from watery necessities such as public baths and washing places to paving, lighting and education. It is difficult to imagine how Lichfield would have fared without it.

Thus within the space of a generation (and two bishops) a new Lichfield was born. It seems likely that the church of St Mary's was erected

11   *The Crucifix Conduit, which stood at the gate to the Friary until 1927. Lichfield's conduits were, quite literally, a talking-point, where news was passed on and quarrels started. In the 1870s the* Lichfield Mercury *even called its gossip column 'Under the Conduit Clock'.*

during this town planning phase, its position in the middle of the market place (buildings later squeezed it on the southern side) reflecting the mixture of spiritual and economic concerns that were transforming Lichfield. Putting a church in the market square, however, made little commercial sense, as it considerably reduced the space available for stalls. As a result a second market place was established at Greenhill, with a further release of burgage plots to go with it. The holding of a weekly market was only the first step in commercial growth. In 1307 the bishop was given the right to hold a fair on Whit Monday (which still survives) and the 14 days after, and this was followed by other fairs in September and November.

We might want to ask whether Bishop Clinton's scheme was a success. The fact that the modern city still preserves so well the outline of its 13th-century predecessor suggests that it did not grow or develop as energetically as its founder might have wished. Even in 1298, when a survey was made of the bishop's estates, only 283 burgage plots were occupied and paying the annual 12d. rent, along with three and a half plots reserved rent free for the friary. A rough count suggests that the take-up rate on available burgages

12 *The cathedral and Minster Pool from Harwood's* Antiquities of the Church and City of Lichfield *(1806). The houses of the residentiary canons were concentrated on the south side of the close, with gardens running down to the pool. Such pleasant views are now enjoyed by the archdeacon of Lichfield and by the bishop, who moved house from the north side of the close to the south in 1953.*

13 *The upper courtyard of the Vicars' Close, much of which dates back to the 15th century. The land was given to them by Bishop Langton in 1314, but the vicars had to build the timber-framed houses themselves. This was one of the few parts of the close not to be damaged in the Civil War or subsequently by wealthy tenants wanting to 'modernise'. Such later improvements can be seen in the lower courtyard.*

was less than 50 per cent, allowing the ambitious to expand into adjacent plots, and the more ambitious still to stay away altogether. Evidence of such double plots can still be seen on the city's streets today. Nevertheless, the annual rent that the bishop drew from the development was £14 6s. 8d. (boosted by another £6 from market tolls), money that he would not have had otherwise, but hardly riches beyond measure.

There was, however, an early opportunity to think again. In 1291 Lichfield experienced a major fire, resulting in the loss of the friary, the churches and (as a couple of early chronicles report) almost the whole town. In the aftermath a new wave of development and building began. Bishop Walter Langton (1296-1321) is principally remembered for adding a lady chapel to the cathedral and for erecting a new bishop's palace, but his activities were not confined to the cathedral close. A causeway (though only about seven feet wide) cutting across the Minster Pool was built at this time and this no doubt stimulated work on the approach road, now called St John Street. As with the inhabitants of Lichfield today, roadworks were a constant menace to their 13th-century ancestors.

Nevertheless, road improvements were becoming necessary, for Lichfield's position on the main routes from London to Carlisle, and from Bristol to Doncaster, as well as the pulling-power of its market, were adding considerably to the traffic passing through. In 1299 the king gave permission for tolls to be levied on all goods entering the city, the income to go towards paving the streets and fortifying the close. These tolls give us a good idea of what livestock and foodstuffs were finding their way to market, and what raw materials were needed by local industries. There were, of course, plenty of horses, cattle, pigs and sheep, but also a wide range of fish, from fresh salmon and eels to herrings and conger. Salted and fresh meat was arriving too, as well as honey, garlic and oil. We know from two surviving 14th-century accounts that wine was being imported too, coming by boat from Bristol to Bridgnorth and then overland from there. As for the raw materials being bought by the manufacturers, they reflect the needs of any medieval community, but there are signs of specialist trades too. The tanners needed skins, as did the glovers and parchment makers; the blacksmiths and carters required nails and horseshoes, while the rope makers had need of web and hemp. But the increasing importance of the cloth trade in Lichfield is reflected in the quantities of fleeces and woollen felt, worsted and silk that were coming in, as well as the woad, verdegris and alum needed by the dyers.

The trade in wool and cloth was connecting Lichfield to a wider market. We know of merchants from London visiting the city in 1305, and that a merchant from Amiens, Walter de Spagny, was a resident in the 1260s. One local product appears to have been in particular demand: 'Lichfield kersey', a coarse woollen cloth principally used in making trousers, was being asked for by name in the Isle of Man in the early 16th century. As for the leather workers, they were especially active in the Stowe Street area, but references to cobblers do turn up across the city. A large dump of cobbler's waste, spanning 150 years of shoemaking in the city, was found some years back on the site of the Wyrley & Essington Canal. Those involved in tanning and dyeing were dependent on large quantities of water, and their waste is often uncovered in Minster and Stowe Pools. The importance of the leather and cloth trades to Lichfield is also reflected in the street names. Part of the market in the 14th century was known as Cloth or Wool Cheaping, while Market Street itself had earlier been called Robe Street and Saddler Street. In 1380 the poll tax returns list 12 tailors, 11 shoemakers, and two each of glovers, fullers, weavers and skinners. It has to be said, though, that these numbers are far outweighed by the labourers and cottagers engaged in agriculture.

However, by the 1560s the cobblers were numerous enough to have formed a Guild of Corvisers. The ordinances of the guild, dated 1625 though no doubt reflecting earlier concerns too, claimed that unskilled corvisers and curriers were entering the city to set up business. It was here specified that none might enter the profession without serving a seven-year apprenticeship (or paying £10 to the guild), and that no more than two apprentices could serve a master at any one time. Payments to employees and journeymen were capped, and an excessively competitive attitude between employers was also severely frowned upon. When one member, Thomas Ashmole, called a fellow worker 'a cobbling clown' in 1626 he was fined 3s. 4d. by the guild.

The proximity of the cathedral with its dean and chapter also demanded the presence of specialist craftspeople. It appears that a cathedral city could expect to provide ecclesiastical services for the whole diocese, and anyway the cathedral itself was in constant need of new furnishings. Stonemasons and glaziers were always in demand and, as the bureaucracy of church affairs grew, so did the demand for parchment, a trade that dovetailed neatly into Lichfield's other skills in leather. So too did the making of gloves, something of a status symbol in the Middle Ages, and a common gift between those of

14 *Bore Street in c.1900. It was referred to as Bord Street in the 14th century. Always one of the principal thoroughfares in the town, the street contained six public houses and the only theatre. By this date the original theatre had been supplanted by St James's Hall.*

high rank. Goldsmiths are recorded in the city from the early 13th century, and silversmiths too were operating, though never in the numbers that Coventry boasted. Metalworking was something that towns on the Birmingham Plateau specialised in, and the poll tax returns show that Lichfield was no exception, with a variety of smiths, plumbers, arrow makers and ironmongers. The permission given to the bishop by King Stephen in 1151 to mint coinage established another branch of the metal industry. But it was short-lived and probably small scale: one single 'Shortcross' penny minted in the town survives in the collections of the British Museum.

Other trades, less acceptable in the eyes of the law, also thrived on the presence of so many unattached men in close proximity to the city. Prostitution was a common concern of the consistory court, and the visitation books of the dean and surviving court records show that clerics were not immune to the temptations of the flesh, although it was usually the women who were punished, typically with a fine of one shilling and a whipping. One member of the cathedral clergy, Thomas Coke, was presented in 1461 as having fathered two illegitimate children from one woman in Coventry, and of being visited by another, who had moved into his chamber in the close 'with two gallons of ale'. The dean had to deal with three prostitutes in 1466, including Margaret Throstyll 'who denied none who came to her and every night made so much noise that her neighbours could get no sleep' and one Cecilia 'who boasted that she had been known fourteen times by day and night by members of the Duke of Clarence's household'. She had made, it was alleged, £3 from her considerable exertions.

Beacon Street became especially notorious for brothels as such passing trade increased, for Lichfield was beginning to have considerable political and strategic significance. Every king of England from Edward II to Henry V either visited or stayed in the town. Richard II favoured the place particularly, spending two Christmases in Lichfield and then, less happily, passed through on the way to his death in the Tower in 1399. The two visits could hardly provide a greater contrast in the hapless king's fortunes. In 1397 it is reported that Richard's party consumed no less than 200 tons of wine and 2,000 oxen, and a new hall had to be built in the close to accommodate them. Two years later Richard's party was somewhat depleted, and led by Henry Bolingbroke, who was shortly to depose him. Jean Creton, a French courtier who was accompanying the king, reports the following incident during the company's stay at Lichfield:

> Soon they came to Lichfield, a very fine little city. While they were there King Richard tried to make his escape by letting himself down into the garden at night from a window of the great tower in which they had lodged him. But it was not, I think, God's will that he should scape, for he was spotted and most cruelly forced back into the tower. So from that time onwards there were always ten or twelve armed men guarding him throughout the night, with the result that he hardly slept at all.

In 1303 Bolingbroke made a return visit as Henry IV, summoning knights, squires and yeomen to Lichfield before his campaign against Owen Glendower, whilst in 1485 Lord Stanley received Henry Tudor in the city with military honours, prior to the Battle of Bosworth. Apart from what entertainment they might find in Beacon Street, such visiting parties also required accommodation, and among the earliest inns recorded are the *Swan* in Bird Street (1392), the *Lion* in Market Street (1440) and the *Antelope* and the *Unicorn*, adjoining each other in Bird Street. By the end of the century there were at least another five inns open for business.

The poll tax of 1377 (levied at 4d. a head on all citizens over 14 years) suggests a population in Lichfield of around 1,400 people, only a fifth of the population of Coventry, but the latter was by far the largest urban centre in the Midlands. By now the new town demanded a new tier of government independent of the manorial court. The burgage-holders (burgesses) expected and already received some powers of representation, but this body had remained vague both in its status and authority. Only with the formal establishment of the Guild of St Mary and St John the Baptist by Richard II in 1387 do we have something firmer to go on. In fact the new body was an amalgamation of two existing guilds connected to St Mary's church, and the king was happy to endorse the union for a fee of £30. Both guilds were primarily religious bodies and consisted of both men and women, and the successor was similarly constituted. Led by an elected

15 *Market Street in 1983. The shop frontages of the modern town still indicate the planned character of the medieval town. Some remain 40 feet wide, whilst others were subsequently divided into two 20-feet plots. Similar patterns can be found in cathedral towns in Germany. Market Street (formerly Robe Street and Saddler Street) was always likely to be one of the more desirable locations, because of its proximity to the market.*

committee of a master and 12 wardens (all of whom had to live in Lichfield), the guild was to 'maintain divine service and works of charity and to suppress vice and evil deeds … so that peace, tranquillity, concord and unity should be promoted in that town'. King Richard had much need of all of these in the years after the Peasants' Revolt.

The guild remained in possession of such powers for a little over 200 years, until its suppression in 1548. Principally, of course, it was there to secure the safe passage of its members' souls into the after-life, and as such the guild recruited widely among the local (and not so local) nobility, averaging 100 new members a year by the end of the 15th century. The surviving register of the guild contains the names of some 11,500 members who enrolled in the course of its existence. For the benefit of their souls the institution employed up to five chaplains, who were accommodated in a house called the Priests' Hall at 5 Breadmarket Street, close to St Mary's church, where they attended mass daily. The Georgian façade of the current building conceals

16 *The interior of the cathedral in 1813, showing part of the west door and west window. None of the cathedral's medieval glass survives. The west window was re-glazed in 1666 after the Civil War, while the glass in the Lady Chapel came from the dissolved abbey of Herckenrode in Belgium.*

a timber-framed Tudor dwelling, where the priests once roamed and where the antiquarian, Elias Ashmole, spent his childhood. As for the members themselves, meetings seem initially to have taken place in private houses; the guildhall in Bore Street was only in operation by the early 15th century. Despite its primarily sacramental mission the guild was also much involved in policing the city as well, and the ordinances of 1486 suggest that they came down hard on 'any misruled or ill-disposed persons that suspiciously walketh by night out of due time'. For all the night-walkers, harlots and scolds apprehended, there was a variety of punishments on offer. The pillory awaited them in the market square and the gaol may have been there as well, before it was incorporated into the guildhall building in Bore Street. The cuckstool needed to be near to water, and no doubt many a recalcitrant Lichfield woman was ducked in the Minster Pool.

Thus medieval Lichfield served a variety of masters, no more so perhaps than any medieval town, but more closely focused. The cathedral spires rose up on the far side of the Minster Pool, reminding all that the power of the bishop as lord of the manor still carried weight, and that the dean was keeping a watchful eye on the morals of the townsfolk. The cathedral clergy too were a force to be reckoned with, holding over 200 tenements in the town and 185 holdings in the open fields around it. But the creation of the Guild of St Mary and St John at least suggested that Bishop Clinton's new town had now come of age, and was beginning to enjoy a life of its own. But forces that were gathering far away from this quiet corner of Staffordshire would soon be changing all that.

CHAPTER THREE

Reforming Zeal

Sometime in the 1540s Lichfield received its first *bona fide* tourist. Of course it could be argued that the countless pilgrims who had passed through the place on their way to the shrine of St Chad were a medieval version of the same industry, but the visit of John Leland was purely as a spectator, and to set down on paper what he saw. His account, the most detailed description of Lichfield thus far, is important enough anyway, but particularly so in that it records the city on the brink of considerable changes. The ideological 'Year Zero' that was the Reformation was about to traumatise England as a whole, but its impact would necessarily be all the greater in an ecclesiastical centre such as Lichfield.

Leland's report is too lengthy to quote in its entirety, but let us at least walk alongside him. With the enthusiasm of a well-trained antiquarian Leland launches initially into the question of Lichfield's castle, noting in passing the ditch below Borrowcop Hill, which we referred to in the first chapter. Dismissing the notion of a castle on this site, he writes:

> It is my guess that a more likely location for the original castle would actually have been the enclosure of the palace, which occupies a rather castle-like position.

The speculation is not far off the mark. Once Bishop Langton had finished his fortification of the close, with massive gateways and corner towers, it did indeed give the impression of a castle and is sometimes referred to as such. Little substance remains of this work, though the view from Gaia Lane across the dry moat suggests how formidable it once was. Strong enough, at least, to resist the artillery of the Roundheads a century later.

Having crossed the ditch, John Leland entered the town proper. He goes on:

> The town itself is large and attractive, with three parish churches. St Mary's is an extremely beautiful piece of architecture, which stands right in the market-place.

17 *The gateway to the choristers' house in the close, from the* Gentleman's Magazine *(1773). The master and choristers were assigned a house in the close in 1527 by Bishop Blythe and a gatehouse was built shortly afterwards. The house still stands behind its Georgian façade in the north-west corner of the close. The gateway, however, was demolished in 1772 as part of a general modernisation.*

We have to take Leland's word for this. The present St Mary's bears little resemblance to its medieval predecessor, and even this may have been a rebuilding of one destroyed in the fire of 1291. The church that Leland saw had benefited considerably from the endowments of Thomas Heywood (dean of Lichfield 1457-92), who had paid for a new east window, rood loft and pillars for the nave, and was thus probably at its best. But the under-investment that followed soon took the shine off it. The spire blew down in 1594, fell down once more in 1626 and (believe it or not) collapsed yet again during a service in 1716. The damage incurred on this third occasion was not helped by the worshippers who smashed their way to safety through the stained-glass windows. (Evidently they trusted less in divine providence than did their preacher, who protected himself by putting a cushion on his head.) The result of all this was a complete rebuilding in the 1730s, followed by yet another rebuild in the late 1860s. The heritage centre which now occupies the main portion of the church opened in 1981; it is hoped that it will last as long as the current spire does.

Leland's next remarks concern the Guild of St Mary and St John and the hospital in St John's Street, but he adds nothing to what has been said in the previous chapter. From this he turns his attention to the subject of education, a theme we have not yet touched on. There can be little doubt that some educational provision must have been made for Lichfield's children in the Middle Ages, if only to supply capable singers for the cathedral choir.

A cathedral song school was operating in the close from the 12th century, accommodating both day scholars and boarders. By the 1520s all were living in what appears to have been a purpose-built house on the north side of the close, which received a water supply direct from the conduit. No doubt the master lived there too, for his salary of £2 13s. 4d. (plus an additional 3s. for each boy) hardly allowed him to rent anywhere better. But for anything more than a musical training Lichfield was poorly equipped, and references to grammar masters in the town are rare. This at least seems to be the implication of the claim made in 1495 that:

> … there had not been (according to the canons) any regular instruction of the youth in grammar, gratis, by reason of the insufficiency of the masters and the smallness of their stipends.

All this was to change in 1495 with Bishop Smith's re-foundation of St John's Hospital, which was now to have an educational mission to add to its charitable one. A grammar school (meaning a school where Latin grammar

18 *The old grammar school, from a print published by Thomas Lomax in the 1860s. The sparse population in the playground reflects the reality of recruitment at the time. In 1865 there were only 26 day-boys and 17 boarders. A far cry from its zenith under John Hunter, who had to rent adjoining property to accommodate as many as 100 boarders.*

was taught) was to be supported on the foundation, the schoolmaster receiving an annual salary of £10 and his deputy or usher £2. Both of them were to live in the hospital and 'have no contact with women'. Among the first teachers at the school was the famous Tudor grammarian, Robert Whittinton, who calls himself 'Lichfieldensis' in his earliest publications. As such he is the first famous name connected with the town, who was not a churchman. He claimed the title, somewhat ambitiously, of 'Protovates Angliae' (England's first poet), but the series of grammatical textbooks in Latin that flowed from his pen, although they gave him temporary fame

and fortune, hardly guaranteed a posthumous reputation. Nor, it has to be said, is his *Little Book of Manners for Children* (a translation from Erasmus) much read by the city's children today. Still, the school he taught at survived: the grammar school, and the song school in the close, were to remain Lichfield's only centres of formal education until the middle of the 17th century.

Whether John Leland's description reflects the route of his perambulation is hard to judge, but from St John's Street he next finds himself in the market place:

> There used to be a fine old cross with steps around it in Lichfield market-place. But Dean Denton has recently spent £160 in enclosing the cross within a structure of eight fine arches, surmounted by a round vault, to enable poor market traders to stand in the dry.

19 *Dean Denton's famous market cross from Harwood's* Antiquities of the Church and City of Lichfield *(1806). The cross was destroyed in the Civil War and the stocks seen here may well have been thrown into the Minster Pool, from where they were retrieved in 1680. The bell would have been rung to mark the beginning and end of the day's trading in the market.*

We know from other sources that the structure also carried statues of eight apostles, two brass crucifixes and a bell. Here again Leland was seeing the market cross at its best; had he arrived a century later he would not have seen it at all, the cross being one of the many casualties of Lichfield's involvement in the Civil War. If our guide had stopped to do some shopping – market day was now Wednesday – rather than hurrying off along Dam Street, he would have found that the market too had undergone changes since the 1300s. For one thing the stalls no longer surrounded St Mary's church, but had been squeezed to the north side of it by new building, of which the guildhall was a major example. Within what was left of the market different areas had become associated with particular products. The butchers operated on the Conduit Street side, while the north side of the square specialised in salt. The area to the west of the church had become known as Women's Cheaping, where female traders gathered. No doubt most of the stock on sale in the market was local produce, but this was not solely the case. We know, for example, that in 1532 salmon, herrings, oil and honey were being sent to Lichfield from Ireland.

Leland was clearly impressed by the three pools which still divided the town from the cathedral close: Upper Pool, near which the soap-makers tended to congregate, Minster or Bishop's Pool, where eels swam and the bishop's swans sailed serenely until their presence was required on the banqueting table, and Stowe Pool, with its good stock of fish and impressive length. The silting and stagnation which would later turn much of Stowe Pool into a boggy marsh was still some way off. And so he passed into the close:

> There are very fine prebendal houses in the close built by several differ-
> ent men, and there is a good house for the choristers recently erected by
> Bishop Blythe … Thomas Heywood built the library in the north-western
> quarter of Lichfield Cathedral. The pride of the cathedral church is the
> architecture of its west front, which is exceptionally lavish and beautiful.
> It has three stone spires.

Few would disagree with Leland's opinion here. Even today the close is an architectural gem, with more buildings listed at Grade I (three) or Grade II* (12) than most towns can boast in their entirety. In fact the present close has more variety and a greater architectural range than the one Leland visited, which had seen considerable construction work, but spread over little more than 200 years. The most dominant feature, apart from the cathedral itself, would certainly have been the bishop's palace, built between 1304 and 1314 by Bishop Langton, and occupying the north-eastern corner of the close where the cathedral school now stands. The great hall was one of the largest half dozen in the country, with a massive carved and gilded roof and walls decorated with paintings of the life of Edward I, who died just as the palace was being built. The palace had its ceremonial and ecclesiastical functions (reflected in its halls, guest rooms and chapel), but it also addressed more mundane needs too, with a bakehouse, granary, salthouse, buttery and stables. The bishop, like any secular lord, shared his residence (if not his living room) with sheep, poultry, pigs, pigeons and horses.

Next to the bishop's palace (to the west) stood the deanery, as it still does, though the house we see today reflects the changing architectural and domestic tastes of many later deans. Only when we move into the north-western corner of the close can we find a range of buildings that Leland and their Tudor occupants would recognise. Here the vicars choral had their houses, arranged around two courtyards, much like an Oxbridge college. The life of the vicars was indeed rather collegiate; they received an allowance to cover meals and shared a common hall (later converted into a private residence by Erasmus Darwin) and chapel. Dean Heywood even provided them with a sickbay. On the downside their domestic lives were strictly controlled. The rules stated that they were to behave themselves at table, and not to refuse any food set down before them; they could not gamble in hall, except for ale, and their rooms were to be kept free of women and hunting dogs.

Other groups of cathedral officials and clergy could also be found nearby. The young choristers and their master, as Leland says, were presented with their own house in the close in 1527 and, given their need to attend services throughout the night, this was clearly desirable. Chantry priests celebrated masses and obits in the cathedral for those who had left money or land for that purpose. By the 1530s there were 17 such chantries and up to 17 priests performed this daily routine from six till ten in the morning, followed by a high mass and another for travellers. They too were accommodated in a 'college' on the south side of the close, with a garden running down to the pool. It would be difficult to estimate the total number of residents in the close, but with the addition of servants, kitchen staff and wardens it is likely to have been in the hundreds, a substantial number in a town of 2,000 people.

Last but not least is the cathedral itself. The building work which had been on-going since the 1250s had long since been completed, no doubt releasing funds for other projects around the close and the town. Only general maintenance and repair of fabric had been necessary since the end of the 14th century. John Leland picks out two major features, as we probably would today, and both were substantially completed in the 40 years or so between 1290 and 1330. Perfect timing, in fact, for the Black Death would doubtless have put a stop to such work. Facing the main entrance the visitor would have seen a screen of perhaps 64 statues, with another group of around 20 below the two towers. This had become the popular way to fill the west front of cathedrals, and the scheme at Lichfield is not dissimilar to those at Wells and Exeter. As such it mixed high-minded piety with hard-nosed realism. At ground level stood the 12 apostles, the four evangelists, Moses and Aaron, Christ and the Virgin. Above them were arrayed the kings of England. Since there had been only nine or ten since the Conquest, and there were 24 niches, these may have been kept company by pre-Conquest kings or (more likely) kings of Israel. Celia Fiennes, a visitor to the city in the 1690s, calls them 'kings of Jerusalem'. Above them stood two rows of prophets and judges, and higher still a selection of patriarchs. All in all, a time-line in stone, and a useful way to remind oneself who had succeeded Henry II.

Much of this statuary was damaged in the Civil War, but it was 1820 before reinforcements began to arrive, carved by Joseph Harris of Bath. The remaining empty niches were filled by a local sculptor, Robert Bridgeman, in the 1870s, with the exception of Queen Victoria, whose likeness was carved by her daughter, Princess Louise. Charles II had arrived in the 1680s to fill the central niche above the west window, politically correct at the time, but somewhat dubious theologically. He was replaced by Christ and relegated to ground level by the more pious Victorians, though the king still waits expectantly for promotion by the south door.

The three spires, so distinctive a feature of the Lichfield skyline, were also in place by the 1320s, and remained so until the Parliamentarians used the central spire as target practice. Luckily the number was only reduced to two temporarily. Reconstruction began almost immediately and by April 1666 Bishop Hackett was writing: 'we have in Lichfield the stateliest spire and the goodliest window in stone to the west that is in England. I would they were paid for.' He recognised, as countless others have done since, that Lichfield was in a sense defined by its three spires. Daniel Defoe, writing in the 1720s, considered them superior to any in Europe. Quite who first dubbed them 'the ladies of the vale' is not easy to uncover. Francis Mundy called them this in

20 *The west front of the cathedral, engraved by Daniel King in 1656. The 15th-century cathedral library can be seen on the far left. The richness of the exterior (which seems to have survived the Reformation intact) belied the relative poverty of the institution. In 1625 the Chancellor of Salisbury asked King James for the deanery of Salisbury, Rochester 'or at least of poor Lichfield, which is hardly worth £100 per annum'.*

1776, but a generation earlier Honora Sneyd, a friend of Anna Seward's, had already referred to the spires as 'the ladies of the valley'.

The inside of the building would have given the impression of considerable colour and richness, especially after the efforts of the energetic Dean Heywood, who had paid for frescoes and stained-glass in the chapter house, and a great stone screen across the entrance to the Lady Chapel. In addition he paid for a new organ and the casting of the great Jesus Bell which summoned townsfolk to Friday evening prayers. Safely gathered inside, the people of Lichfield would have been rubbing shoulders with the great bishops and deans whose ambition and wealth had driven their city forward. All were now silent beneath their stone canopies, there to remain until the last trump summoned them. The tomb of Dean Heywood in the south transept was among them, sculpted in the popular fashion of the 1470s, richly dressed in his vestments above, and a naked cadaver below, to remind onlookers of the vanity of it all. Finally, standing on a marble table in the Lady Chapel, was the reason for Lichfield's existence in the first place: the richly decorated shrine of St Chad, now in his eighth century of residence. How the town had changed in all those years.

But soon it was all to change again. At the accession of Henry VIII to the English throne Lichfield's very own laureate, Robert Whittinton, had composed Latin verses, heralding the return of a golden age, a conceit he then recycled in a similar poem for Thomas Wolsey. As it turned out, the promised golden age would not be exactly the one anticipated. The reformation of religion that swept across Lichfield came in waves, a first wave in the 1530s, then another in the 1540s, followed by a temporary reversal of the tide in the 1550s. That, in brief, was the effect of the reigns of Henry and his two children, Edward and Mary.

The Reformation was a political act, rejecting the interference of Rome in domestic concerns and asserting the independence of the English Church. But it was also ideological and theological, denying the concept of purgatory, or the power of relics, prayers or obits to shepherd the soul safely through it. Inevitably then, the shrine of Chad was the first to bear the brunt of the new world order. It was said that the shrine brought in an annual income of £400 to the cathedral. In 1538 it was gone, the jewels and ornaments seized for the royal coffers. The remains of Chad himself, as we have seen, went walkabout.

Down in the town the Franciscan friary was about to undergo the same fate. It was handed over on 7 August 1538 to the Bishop of Dover, who wrote to Cromwell that 'it is more in debt than all the stuff that belongs to it will pay ...'. The rent, it seems, had not been paid for five years. A deliberate underestimate, this, for the dispersal sale that followed brought in considerable sums, even though the fixtures and fittings were available at a knock-down price. The copes and vestments sold for £2, the glass for 3s. and a holy water stoup for 1s. 8d. Whatever sympathy the townsfolk might have felt for the now homeless friars, there was no shortage of takers. A syndicate of eight men bought the buildings, on the understanding that they should 'deface the tower, cloister, choir and church' within four months and pull down the lot inside three years. As for the land, it was snapped up by a property speculator and then transferred to Gregory Stonyng, who happened to be the master of St Mary's Guild. An inside job, one imagines. Since the law had not stipulated its destruction, Stonyng and his wife were able to move into 'an inn called le Bishop's Lodging', parts of which still survive on the south side of The Friary. The road cuts across what was clearly a large site – the church itself being over 200 feet long – and follows the southern edge of the cloister. And so Lichfield's only monastic institution bit the dust, mourned perhaps, but hardly missed. Let one gravestone from the friary cemetery that turned up in building work in 1746 provide its epitaph. Undated and in Latin, the grave was clearly that of a local merchant, attracted (as many were) to commit his body to the good friars for burial. The master of St John's at the time, Theophilus Buckeridge, turned the lines into English verse and the *Gentleman's Magazine* published them:

> Richard the Merchant here extended lies,
> Death, like a stepdame, gladly closed his eyes;
> No more he trades beyond the burning zone,
> But happy rests beneath this sacred stone;
> His benefactions to the Church were great,
> Tho' young, he hastened from this blest retreat;
> May he, though dead, in trade successful prove
> St Michael's merchant in the realms above.

The *Valor Ecclesiasticus*, Henry's audit of church property, had estimated Lichfield cathedral's wealth as worth £1,408 8s. 4d., well down the league table of cathedrals. But, as a secular foundation, Lichfield was able to hold on to it. Whatever theological direction the state was taking it would still need cathedrals. Lichfield's sister church in Coventry, of course, was not so lucky. As a priory it had to be dissolved and destroyed. So, although the title

Coventry and Lichfield survived in the diocesan title, it now had only one cathedral. In the light of all those political battles in the past, some of the Lichfield canons might be excused for feeling rather smug: the Reformation clearly had its compensations.

But they were not out of the wood yet, not by a long way. The Chantries Act of 1547 spelled the end for all those chantry chapels and altars scattered about the church. It meant redundancy for the 17 chantry priests and, most important of all, the sale of all the properties and lands that had supported them. Once more the London speculators were on hand to relieve them of all such real estate, and to make sure that it found a good home. (Property speculators from the capital are not only a feature of the modern world.) The chief beneficiaries of these transactions were, ironically, the Levesons of Wolverhampton, who were Catholics to a man. The chantry priests' house in the close was snapped up too, but it found its way into the hands of Dean Richard Walker, who used the rent to endow the grammar school.

The *South East Prospect* of the Friary Lich: *as it Appear'd Sep: 10, 1782.*

21   *What remained of the Friary complex in 1782. Building was still in progress on the eve of the Reformation, and Gregory Stonyng enlarged the 'Bishop's Lodging' once he obtained the lease. A fireplace from his house can still be seen in the children's section of the library, which now occupies most of the site.*

The Chantries Act signalled the end of the Guild of St Mary and St John too, since it effectively operated as a chantry for its members. But here there was significant compensation. Since the guild had also been the town's government it was forcefully and successfully argued that Lichfield would be left ungoverned unless a replacement was provided. And so – a key moment in Lichfield's history – the borough was incorporated by a charter of Edward VI in 1548 and made a city. When coupled with the bishop's resignation of his manorial rights in the same year, it must have seemed that Lichfield's rise to independent borough, city and corporation status (the first in Staffordshire) was nothing short of meteoric. Nor did the former holdings of the guild entirely disappear. The guildhall remained in the corporation's hands and much of the land as well, although deals had to be struck to secure it. Bolstered by a series of later royal charters, and a few adjustments to the rules for choosing the bailiffs, the city was to be governed by this body for the next 300 years, until the Municipal Corporations Act of 1835.

Yet still the Reformation rolled on. In 1549 the new corporation was having to sell off the plate and altar cloths from St Michael's and St Mary's and was using some of the proceeds to pay for Cranmer's new prayer book. On the other side of town things were looking decidedly worse. Royal agents arrived in January 1553 to take away vestments from the cathedral and, perhaps misjudging the size of the task, returned in May with a wagon. They removed the rest of the copes and mitres and silver vessels, after first defiantly pouring the consecrated oil on the ground in front of two horrified canons. Perhaps the agents told the canons that the lightning which had struck the bell tower in 1550 was proof that God was with them in all this.

There was, however, one temporary blip in the creation of a Protestant state. In 1553, shortly after the stripping of the altars in the cathedral, the Catholic Queen Mary ascended the throne. Service books, chasubles and tunics came mysteriously out of the woodwork and the old order was restored, albeit temporarily. Worries that the city's new-found status would be lost were allayed by a new charter of 1553, granted (said the rubric) for 'the diligent industry and faithful service' given by the corporation in Mary's struggle for the throne. As it was, there was never enough time for a full restoration of Catholic rites. Mary was not a well woman, and six years after her accession she died, leaving the way for her sister, the Protestant Elizabeth, to turn the tide back again.

The changes that resulted from the accessions of Mary and Elizabeth were probably more a matter of personnel than doctrine. However generous the Henrician and Edwardian reforms had been to minor members of the old order, pensioning them off to keep them quiet – the guild chaplains had each received a pension of £6 13s. 4d. and one of them was then re-employed as vicar of St Mary's – it was essential that the figureheads toed the party line. Laurence Saunders, newly appointed divinity lecturer at the cathedral in Marian days, was burned at Coventry for back-sliding tendencies, while John Ramridge, the Catholic dean left high and dry by Mary's early demise, voluntarily took himself into exile, only to be murdered in Flanders. His passing opened the door for a Marian exile, Laurence Nowell, to return in his stead. Nowell would at least have appreciated his new position; he was an unswerving Protestant, a noted antiquarian and a scholar of Anglo-Saxon.

Quite how the average Lichfeldian felt about all these ideological changes is a question historians continue to agonise over, if only because they can never be in a position to provide a complete answer. On the plus side Lichfield had now fully come of age as an city. From being in many ways under the thumb of the bishop, it now had complete control of its own finances and boasted a new range of official personnel such as recorder, steward and sheriff, who presided over the new county court. The fact that the leading members of the old guild had instantly become the leading members of the new corporation – two bailiffs and 24 burgesses – would hardly have come as a surprise to anyone. That was how politics worked.

22   Milley's Hospital on Beacon Street. The almshouse was originally founded in the 15th century by Bishop Heyworth, but was re-built and re-founded in 1504 by Thomas Milley, a canon of the cathedral. At his death in the following year Milley also left 50 shillings to be distributed in bread to the poor.

On the negative side, the dissolution had clearly severed the age-old links between town, church and country. The new landlords in the surrounding countryside were no longer as closely associated with the life of the close and the town as they once had been, and the chantry holdings at least suffered from neglect. The site of the former friary was described as 'wasteland' in 1552, and Bishop Overton said of Lichfield in 1575 that 'it is not the city that it hath been ...'. Change is not something that many embrace willingly and the bishop may have had a particular axe to grind, but it seems undeniable that the spending power of the clergy, upon which Lichfield had come to rely, was not what it was. The economic recession that hit England in the middle of the 16th century cannot have been unrelated to these changes.

There were cultural changes to swallow as well. Many of the folk traditions and festivities we associate with 'Merry England' were too closely linked with the old order to continue for long. The custom of appointing a 'boy bishop' (presumably one of the choristers) on Holy Innocents' Day, as a light-hearted reversal of ecclesiastical roles, was one such, as was the Whitsun procession from neighbouring parishes to bring 'Chad farthings'. Surprisingly, there is no evidence of mystery plays being performed at Lichfield, but this

23   *A box of bower cakes, ready for distribution to eager Lichfield children in 1908. Stebbing Shaw explains that during the ceremony 'those who answer to their name are invited into the bower, and are regaled with cold hanged beef, stewed pruins, cakes, wine and ale'. The event probably dates back to the 12th century, but is now of purely ceremonial significance.*

may reflect the relative smallness of the town and the lack of trade guilds (who traditionally sponsored the plays) in the medieval period. The bishop had his own troupe of minstrels who regularly played at the fairs, but they too disappear with the Reformation.

Nevertheless, one medieval tradition did survive as it still does today. Quite how much the Bower Procession of recent times reflects the medieval version is difficult to say, for the earliest known description only dates from the 1690s. Celia Fiennes describes the ceremony like this:

> They have in this town a Custom at Whitsuntide ye Monday and Tuesday Call'd ye green Bower feast, by which they hold their Charter. The

Baillif and Sheriff assist at ye Cerimony of dressing up Baby's with garlands of flowers and Carry it in procession through all ye streetes, and then assemble themselves at ye Market place and so go on in a solemn procession through the great streete to a hill beyond ye town where there is a large Bower made with greens in which they have their feast. Many lesser Bowers they make about for Conveniency of ye Whole Company and for selling fruite Sweetmeetes and Gingerbread which is a Chief Entertainment.

There is no doubt that the origins of the Bower procession lay in the manorial customs of much earlier days. By the late 15th century it had become customary, if not essential, to maintain a watch during the Whitsun Fair, when there was an increased risk of trouble. At the beginning of the fair an inspection of the watch was made by the bishop's steward and bailiff, a bower of birch trees being erected at Greenhill for him to sit beneath. After inspection the watch marched proudly through the town. From the earliest period the event mixed formal ceremony with festivities: the bishop's minstrels were there and ale flowed freely. With the transfer of manorial powers to the corporation in 1548 the event became instead a very visible symbol of the borough's status and that of its elected officials. One imagines that the procession would have included the sheriff, bailiffs and constables. Ironically, the parade described by Anna Seward in 1796, which included 'gaudy morris dancers', and 'emblematic figures and garlands carried on poles' was probably more 'medieval' than the event had ever been. Such are the powers of tradition.

Lichfield's new-found civic confidence had an early opportunity to display itself when Queen Elizabeth spent a week in the city in August 1575. In earlier centuries such royal celebrations would have taken place almost exclusively in the close. Now it was the city itself that was on display. The market place was paved, and the market cross and guildhall were repaired and re-painted. The bailiffs' accounts include a payment of £5 to Mr Cartwright, 'that should have made the Oracion', suggesting that he did not do so. No great loss for the Queen, who had heard a hundred such speeches before. Equally cryptic is the payment to William Hollcroft 'for kepynge Madde Richard when her Majestie was here'. One wonders whether Richard was a loose cannon among the more regular canons. The visit also gave Lichfeldians an early opportunity to see the first of the great Elizabethan theatre companies. A payment of 8s. 8d. to the Earl of Warwick's players suggests that they followed the Queen from her previous engagement at Kenilworth.

24 *The Guildhall in 1838. It was entirely rebuilt ten years later. The charter of 1664 stipulated that on St James's Day (25 July) the brethren should elect two bailiffs and a sheriff 'and upon refusal to serve, should have power, at their discretion, to fine the person refusing, and commit him till the fine be paid ...'. It was alleged that reluctant candidates were sometimes chosen as a devious means of fund-raising.*

There were only 30 years separating the Queen's visit to Lichfield from that of John Leland, but much had altered in that time. The annual Bower procession and Whitsun fair provided the reassurance that the new Lichfield had not entirely lost its links with the past, but a far more tumultuous and damaging century was just on the horizon. When the Quaker, George Fox, visited the city in 1651 after his release from Derby gaol he had a nightmarish vision of the streets flowing with blood. 'Woe to the bloody city of Lichfield!' he cried, walking barefoot through the streets. During the 17th century Lichfield saw more than its fair share of religious fanatics. George Fox might have interpreted his vision as a distant memory of Amphibalus and the early Christian martyrs, but it could equally be read as a premonition.

CHAPTER FOUR

The Bloody City of Lichfield

Few women have so far found a place in our story, and those that have were not as good as they might have been. An inevitable result, it must be said, of centuries dominated by men and of a town monopolised by unmarried ones. Joyce Lewes of Mancetter might have wished for the same obscurity, but she was not to be so lucky. In 1556 or 1557 the unfortunate woman (a niece of the Protestant martyr, Hugh Latimer) was burnt in Lichfield as a heretic, her grim end witnessed by the sheriff and the wives of a number of Lichfield's prominent citizens, including Margaret Biddulph and Joan Lowe. They offered, it is said, comfort to the dying woman. The 16th century was a warm time for heretics, and there were three such executions in Lichfield alone.

Nor were the burnings over with the death of Joyce Lewes or even of Queen Mary. There was to be one more, the last in England, and a sign perhaps that the tension between Catholic and Protestant had been replaced by distrust between orthodoxy and nonconformity. This, in many ways, was to be the theme of the next chapter in Lichfield's history.

In doctrinal terms Staffordshire was arguably the most divided county in England. The area in and around Wolverhampton was widely regarded as a 'nest of papists', and families such as the Giffards of Chillington firmly held onto their Catholic faith in spite of what the government said. Lichfield, as we would expect of a cathedral town, was a centre of orthodoxy and Anglicanism, reinforced by the bishop, the dean and their courts. But elsewhere, the more radical leanings associated with Puritanism were beginning to make in-roads. This was especially true around Burton-upon-Trent and, although it would not be until the 1640s that such views became widespread, they were evident in the area from the 1570s. It was, in a sense, up to the bishop of Lichfield and Coventry as to whether he wanted to make an issue of it. Richard Neile (1610-14) was a highly orthodox and authoritarian bishop and he did indeed want to make an issue of it.

One of the consequences of Protestantism was to bring the individual believer into much closer touch with the word of God, delivered by the preacher or read in an English bible. As Calvinist beliefs grew there were a number of individuals who sought to cut out the middle man entirely and imbibe their inspiration directly. Such a one was Edward Wightman, who began to attend the Burton 'exercises', as these unofficial Puritan gatherings were called. Compared with Wightman, the other Puritans who participated were as moderate as choirboys. Wightman summarily rejected the Trinity, infant baptism, the Incarnation, the creeds, the marriage of priests and indeed almost all of what you might think of as Christianity. Probably the best way to deal with Wightman was to ignore him: persecution would only make him worse. But when he sent a manuscript to the King, claiming for himself prophetic powers through the agency of the Holy Spirit, it was clear that something had to be done. Bishop Neile had little choice but to summon him to the consistory court, where cross-questioning by Neile and his chaplain, William Laud (the future Archbishop of Canterbury), only served to show just how heretical Wightman was. Madness, it seems, was no excuse. And so on 9 March 1612 there arrived the writ from King James, demanding:

> … that thou cause the said Edward Wightman to be committed to the fire in some public and open space below the city aforesaid, before the people, and the same Edward Wightman in the same fire cause really to be burned in the detestation of the said crime and for the manifest example of all Christians …

Traditionally it is said that the sentence was carried out in the market place, though the wording of the king's writ and the ever-present danger of sparks igniting nearby buildings suggests that a site outside the town centre would have been preferred. The exact location mattered little to Wightman. No doubt the Burton mercer held his beliefs deeply and (as the rubric put it) 'obstinately', but burning faggots do tend to concentrate the mind. No sooner had the fire been lit than Wightman signalled that he was ready and willing to recant, the crowd pulling away the burning wood to release him. Wightman was then taken back to prison to await another appointment with the bishop. Some weeks later, the warmth from the fire now a distant memory, he returned to court, more obstinate and heretical than ever. There would be no third chance. On Saturday 11 April, the day between Good Friday and Easter Sunday, Edward Wightman perished in the fire, 'blaspheming to the end'. He was the last heretic to be burnt in England, and a rare example of one who was burnt twice.

Once the smoke from Wightman's pyre had cleared, Lichfield life returned to something like normality. The city was continuing to grow, albeit slowly, kept in check by the frequent appearance of plague. The one which raged through 1593 and 1594 was especially severe, resulting in the death of some 1,100 people in the city, perhaps half the population. A further 821 died in the outbreak of 1646. Gregory King (1648-1712), one of the pioneers of statistics in England, applied his new art to the population in 1695, and calculated the total of people in the close and city at 3,038. A century later the number would only have risen by a further 700 or so. In terms of trade and occupation there was little to distinguish the 17th century from the one before it. Lichfield's once prosperous capping industry had certainly declined (as it had in Stafford), but the growth in the metal trade had more than made up for this. Guilds of smiths, farriers, bakers and butchers were in existence at least from the 1570s, and formal associations of dyers, weavers and leather workers show that these industries were still thriving as well. Their annual feasts and celebrations provided welcome trade for the growing service industry that supplied food and drink. It was indeed a cause of complaint that the number of inns and alehouses in Lichfield was causing 'much decay in the place'.

Nevertheless, surviving probate inventories – lists of possessions attached to wills – serve to remind us that this was still essentially an agricultural area. In the period up to 1680 husbandry remains the commonest single occupation, far outnumbering the next largest profession, that of innkeeper. Such inventories give us a rare glimpse inside the houses of Lichfield's 17th-century inhabitants, and an indication of how life was lived far from the world of Civil War or consistory court. Julian Stonynge (1618), for example, had 'a pair of clavicalls' in his bedroom, though the 'holland sheet to lay uppon a woman in childbed' might have been much more useful. Lisle Stotesbury (1671) who lived in the close, on the other hand, possessed no fewer than three guitars and four lutes, but (at least according to the inventory) no furniture. In general, however, the inventories from this period demonstrate the close relationship between trade and home life. The house of Dennis Napper (1660) may have been filled with the usual pestles, pots and warming pans, but the 'one thousand and a half brickes' and 'three thousand tyles' in his yard show that he was a builder. The chambers of Samuel Newboult, apothecary (1666), may have contained furniture and utensils to the value of around £23, but it was the stock in his cellar (liquorice, tobacco and vinegar) and shop (turmeric and treacle and ambergris) that lifts his estate to the value of £74. Newboult's wares, along with those of another apothecary, John Parker (1655), who traded under the sign of 'the Naked Boy', show that those who could afford it now had easy access to the spices and oils of the Orient. The property of Anne Smaldridge (1679) in Sandford Street also displays that distinctive mixture of the exotic and the mundane. The quantities of madder, sumach, red wood and copperas show her trade to be that of a dyer of cloth, but the 14 yards of red and brown cloth in the great chamber also indicate that she stored her stock all over the house. She also owned two pigs, two cows and two horses.

But for four years in the 1640s such domestic peace would be a luxury few would be able to enjoy. Storm clouds were gathering at Westminster and Lichfield was about to enter the most traumatic period of its history.

There is not the space here to rehearse the full background to the civil war that was about to engulf all four nations of the British Isles. Suffice to say that it concerned the legislative independence of Parliament, the tax raising powers of the king, the nature of the state religion and the control of the army. Ultimately it would be a question of who governed Britain, a matter that could not be settled then, nor since. But the Revolution or Civil War (historians differ in their nomenclature) was as much a matter of geography as history. For much of the 1640s there were effectively two parliaments, one at Westminster and another based around King Charles I at Oxford. The south and east of the country tended to favour Parliament; the west and north to support the King. The Midlands itself was a patchwork of conflicting loyalties – Coventry and Birmingham declaring for Parliament, Oxford and Worcester for the Crown.

But these simple generalisations can be pressed too far. Conflicting religious beliefs and class divisions made the situation far more fluid than this. In Lichfield, for example, there was a broad swathe of opinion within the corporation that supported the parliamentary cause, while the close inevitably fell behind the Crown. The local gentry on the whole were royalists, led by Sir Richard Dyot, whose family owned estates to the north of the city and a house in Sadler Street, and whose ancestors filled the vaults of St Mary's church. As for Lichfield's members of parliament, they were a mixed bag, and even nobility is no accurate indication of loyalty here. One of the two representatives in the Long Parliament of 1640 was Sir Walter Devereux, son of the Earl of Essex who was beheaded by Elizabeth for treason in 1601. Sir Walter became a key military leader on the parliamentary side. But what was clear in all this was that it would be in Middle England that the war (and many an election since that time) would be decided.

There may have been some Lichfeldians who were hoping that the war would pass them by, as had many wars before this. The letter that arrived from the King on 17 October 1642, requesting arms – 'musketts, pykes, corslitts, swords or weapons' – as well as donations in money or plate, was an early indication that this was not going to be so. But Lichfield was not in the giving mood. A public meeting at the Guildhall sent Sir Richard Dyot on an embarrassing mission to Charles to convey the city's blunt refusal. At least Sir Richard was able to hand over his own plate in compensation, together with a troop of horse that he had raised in the city. Their first taste of action was at Edgehill on 23 October. Sir Richard himself was too old to take part, but that did not prevent his subsequent arrest and imprisonment at Coventry.

In a war that moved rapidly across the country Lichfield was always going to be a place of some significance. The size of the city was of less importance than its strategic position on the routes from London to Shrewsbury and from Bristol to York. But who would seize this opportunity first? This question was answered in December 1643, when a troop of around 300 royalist soldiers, led by the Earl of Chesterfield, entered the city and established a garrison, as other royalists were so doing in Stafford and Dudley. Unlike these other two, Lichfield did not have a castle, nor did it have walls. It did, however, have the next best thing to a castle, at least in terms of defensibility. The cathedral close, courtesy of its powerful medieval bishops, had walls, towers, moat and gates as impregnable as any castle. And so, probably by the following month, the drawbridges were lifted, the portcullis lowered, and the troops inside waited for the inevitable parliamentary riposte.

It came on 1 March. The parliamentary commander in the Midlands was Robert Greville, 2nd Lord Brooke, among whose possessions was Warwick Castle, which had already been garrisoned for Parliament. Lord Brooke had been at the Battle of Edgehill, and had spent the last six months cleaning up in Warwickshire. Now came the command to move into Staffordshire, and he arrived at Lichfield with a force of about 1,200 men and some cannon. Lichfield was hardly in a position to resist an army of this size, and probably

25 *Robert Greville, 2nd Lord Brooke (1608-43), who led the first assault on Lichfield close. On 2 March 1643, wearing 'a plush cassack, with a head piece of steele on, having before his face five barrs of steele gilt', he left his lodgings in Market Street to supervise operations, never to return. What is claimed to be his armour is still displayed at Warwick Castle.*

many in the city would not have wanted to do so anyway. What fighting there was had subsided by 2 March, leaving Lord Brooke in command of the city, but facing the blank, unyielding wall of the cathedral close. The day was, as those inside no doubt realised, the ancient feast day of St Chad.

Given Lord Brooke's intimate knowledge of castles, one might have expected a subtle approach to the problems of siege warfare, but it appears that patience was not one of his virtues. The army's one piece of serious military hardware – known as a demi-culverin – was drawn into position on Dam Street and, in the absence of any better ideas, the attackers began blasting away at the cathedral gate. The defenders inside could do little more than disrupt the operation by firing back at the gun position.

The event that followed has gone down in the annals of Lichfield history, and, as such, probably contains as much fiction as fact. Traditionally what happened next was that a royalist sniper, from his vantage point on the cathedral tower, spotted Lord Brooke leaning out of a window on Dam Street and shot him through the left eye. The fatal shot has been attributed to one John Dyott, a relation of Sir Richard Dyott, who was (it is said) deaf and dumb. No doubt the eyesight of 'Dumb Dyott' was indeed keen, to compensate for his loss of hearing and speech, but a shot as accurate as this seems almost superhuman, given the quality of the weapons then available. More likely is a chance ricochet or a random shot from a sniper rather closer than this, who may indeed have been the celebrated John Dyott. What is undeniable is that Lord Brooke was hit by a bullet which, as the parliamentary newspaper of the time put it, 'instantly put an end to his life, without speaking a word'. The traditional place of his death is still marked by a plaque on Dam Street.

It was rare, and probably unique in the war thus far, for a commanding officer to be killed before any of his men were and, whatever the diurnal or newspaper said about the attackers' immediate resolve and thirst for revenge, it was likely to have had a seriously debilitating effect on their morale. An instant, and hopefully more fortunate, replacement was necessary. The attackers therefore turned to Sir John Gell, who was leading the parliamentary forces in Derbyshire and Nottinghamshire. Gell's arrival introduced more strategy into the operation, even if it was not rewarded with immediate success. Firstly, to avoid a repeat of the previous miscalculation, the parliamentary army set about assembling what we have now learnt to call a 'human shield' to protect them. Known relatives of those defending the close were rounded up and placed in front of the attackers as they continued their assault on the south gate. Secondly, Gell began preparations for a second assault upon the walls on the north side and upon the west gate, gathering scaling ladders and inflammable material to throw into the close and to set fire to the gate.

Both assaults, it has to be said, were famously unsuccessful, the defenders in the close making sorties to drive back the roundheads from the west gate and setting fire to the climbing equipment. In addition, a royalist force led by Colonel Henry Hastings appeared from Rushall to harry the besiegers. All in all, it had been a pretty bad day for the Revolution.

But all this was to change on 4 March, with the arrival from Coventry of a much larger piece of rocketry. As the antiquarian, Stebbing Shaw, wrote a century later:

> This day came their mortar-piece, which struck the poor citizens into an ague-fit of trembling and gazing at the strangeness thereof, having not seen the like before, and hearing the roundhead soldiers making such bragging bravadoes, and thundering out so many terrible threats, crying nothing but fire and sword would reconcile them.

We must allow Shaw the bias of hindsight – history is usually in the hands of the winners – and recognise that the besiegers now at last had the necessary equipment for heavy bombardment. The mortar in question fired hollow balls of iron almost vertically, the interior packed with gunpowder, which dropped down onto the heads of those within the close. In certain circumstances it was feasible to throw the shells back before the fuse ignited the powder, but it was hardly possible to climb the battlements to do so. So the dreaded mortar was hauled into the garden of Sir Richard Dyott's house in Market Street (the irony of this location being secondary to its strategic position on the south side of Minster Pool) and an unpleasant shower of splintered, exploding iron began to fall upon the cathedral close.

Siege warfare is as much a matter of psychology as of military tactics, and here Sir John Gell had won the battle of minds. By the next day the defenders were ready to talk. More important was that they were ready to listen, for the terms of surrender left little room for bargaining:

> First, that the Earl of Chesterfield should forthwith surrender the garrison called the Close of Lichfield, upon conditions of free quarter to all those within the Close. For all other terms they were to throw themselves upon the mercy of Parliament. Second, that if the Earl would not yield up the garrison on these terms, it would be taken by force of arms.

'Free quarter' allowed the majority of the defenders to disperse of their own free will, only the Earl of Chesterfield, his son and a handful of leading royalists being detained. Thus on Sunday, 5 March, the first siege of Lichfield ended with several bangs and a whimper. The parliamentary troops, led by Colonel Russell, marched triumphantly into the close, and the Earl of Chesterfield was conveyed to the Tower, where he was to remain for the rest of the war. The new occupiers of the close, numbering around 500 men, immediately set about shoring up its defences, for they knew that they were unlikely to have it to themselves for long. Indeed, there was an unsuccessful attempt to wrest it back by Colonel Hastings on 21 March. But this was nothing compared with the force of some 1,200 horse and 400 foot soon to be making its way across Warwickshire, intent on yet another change of ownership in Lichfield close.

In the meantime, apart from their defensive duties, the parliamentary army whiled away their time with a spot of simple vandalism. Quite how extensive that destruction was is a debatable point. There is always a strong tendency to blame Cromwell's troops for every act of iconoclasm, forgetting or ignoring the fact that most of the damage had been done in the previous century. Certainly there are strong grounds for believing that some of the parliamentary leaders would not have been sympathetic to the anglicanism on show in a typical English cathedral, but whether they authorised wholesale looting is another matter. The reporting of the war was in the hands of spin-doctors, who were always seeking to exaggerate the sins of one side and to minimise those of the other. John Vicars, writing in the 1640s, was in no doubt of the enormity of the sacrilege taking place:

> The souldiers were mercifull to the men, yet were they void of all pitty toward the organ-pipes, copes, surpluses, and such like popish trumperies found in the Minster, affoording these no quarter, except quartering and mangling them in peeces.

The antiquarian, Sir William Dugdale, for whom the royal cause was almost as important as the preservation of ancient monuments, was equally horrified by what was taking place in the cathedral:

> They stabled their horses in the body of it, kept courts of guard in the cross-isles; broke up the pavements, polluted the qire with their excrement; everyday hunted a cat with hounds throughout the church, delighting themselves with the eccho from the goodly vaulted roof; and to add to their wickedness, brought a calf into it, wrapt in linnen; carried it to the font; sprinkled it with water; and gave it a name in scorn and derision of the holy sacrament of baptism.

The story of the cathedral's rough treatment was still current when Sir Walter Scott described the last resting-place of his hero, Marmion, in 1808:

> Short is my tale: Fitz-Eustace care
> A pierced and mangled body bare
> To moated Lichfield's lofty pile;
> And there, beneath the southern aisle,
> A tomb, with Gothic sculpture fair,
> Did long Lord Marmion's image bear,
> (Now vainly for its sight you look;
> 'Twas levelled when fanatic Brook
> The fair cathedral storm'd and took;
> But thanks to Heaven and good Saint Chad,
> A guerdom meet the spoiler had!)

Scott would have had an opportunity to see the restored church and hear stories of its rough treatment when he visited Anna Seward in the close in May 1807, though as we can see he did not entirely get his facts right. The two poets shared a mutual admiration and had been in correspondence for some years. Anna's last letter (at least among those published) was to Sir Walter just 12 days before she died, and Scott later edited three volumes of her poetry, 'most of which', he privately confided to a friend, 'is absolutely execrable'. The epitaph which Scott composed for Anna's monument in the same cathedral is rather better.

Some of what he heard of the parliamentary outrages may well have been true, but we must also add that the royalist defenders, in their desperate search for ammunition, had already stripped much of the lead from the roof. Sanctity was little protection in the current climate.

Whatever Colonel Russel's men were up to in the cathedral, they were not up to it for long, for on 8 April Prince Rupert arrived outside the city. As with Lord Brooke's assault in the previous month there was little or nothing to prevent the invading army from entering the town and making preparations for an assault upon the close. Whether the Prince had learnt a lesson from the mistakes of his predecessors, or was simply a more astute military tactician, is unclear, but Rupert surely chose rightly in directing his assault against the north side of the close. Here lay higher ground from which he could direct his artillery more effectively. From a piece of ground still called Prince Rupert's Mound, a number of culverins and demi-culverins rained down cannonballs into the close.

But Colonel Russel was made of sterner stuff than the Earl of Chesterfield, and it was clear that random damage such as this was not going to make him budge. Indeed, Prince Rupert surely recognised that such fire was only part of the 'softening up' process, before the real battle of minds could begin. Perhaps we should call it a battle of mines, for the one sure and certain way to take a castle was to dig under its walls. And the only way for the defenders to prevent it was to dig counter mines, hoping to intercept the sappers before they got too close.

Tunnelling is a dangerous and technically difficult business, but Staffordshire was one place where there was no shortage of personnel skilled in the craft. It took little time for around 50 miners to be recruited from the Cannock coalfields and set to work. Their very appearance, let alone their tunnels, must have given the defenders a certain sinking feeling. Still, their success was to be far from immediate. For one thing, the moat had to be drained of water before mining could begin. After that there came the elaborate game of underground chess, as miner and counterminer sought to out-manoeuvre

26   *The view from Prince Rupert's Mound to the north of Gaia Lane. Here the prince set up his artillery positions in early April 1643. Strategically it was the best place both to plan a siege of the close and at the same time to bombard it. It took Rupert less than a fortnight to force out the parliamentary garrison.*

each other. And even when the royalists at last succeeded in digging under the north-west tower of the close, obtaining enough gunpowder to blow it up was no simple matter either. The logistics of munitions supply were not made any easier by Lichfield's distance from the main royalist headquarters. Most of the powder had to be sent up from Oxford (with the promise that surplus quantities would be returned), supplemented by additional supplies from Tamworth.

Nevertheless, the events of Thursday, 20 April 1643, made all that preparation worthwhile. By dawn Prince Rupert's men had packed five barrels' worth of powder into a cavity beneath the tower, lit the fuse and retired to watch the fireworks. By all accounts the blast was spectacular, smashing a hole in the defences 'wide enough for six men to enter abreast'. It was the first recorded use of a landmine in England.

The explosion was not yet the end, as was once said of a later war, but it was the beginning of the end. Although the roundheads fought on from the houses in the close, their own supplies of ammunition and food were dwindling

27 *Stowe Pool in 1785, showing St Chad's church, Stowe House, Stowe Hill and Johnson's Willow. The tower dates from the 1300s, but the church itself is probably of the 12th century. The church and its surroundings were occupied by Lord Brooke's troops during the first siege of Lichfield in 1643. Here, safely out of range of the royalist snipers, they prepared scaling ladders for the assault upon the north wall of the close.*

fast, and they could no longer keep the attackers at arm's length. That being the case, the terms of surrender, offered and accepted, were remarkably generous:

> Lieutenant Colonel Russel, and all the captains and officers with him, shall march out of the Close tomorrow, being the one-and-twentieth day of this instant Aprill, by ten of the clock in the morning, with four score men and musquetts with flying colours, and four score horsemen with arms belonging to them, and all other persons within the said Close to be at liberty to go whither they please; and for their better and safe conveyance, a free pass or convoy from His Highness, and eleven carts to convey away such goods as belong to any of the officers or soldiers with themselves to the Cittie of Coventrie ...

Thus, after an interregnum of six weeks, Lichfield was safely back in royal hands, so to remain for the next three years. Command of the close

28 *The remains of the west gate into the cathedral close, the scene of a bloody skirmish during the first siege of the close, when the royalists lowered the drawbridge and drove back the attackers. After the final capture of the close in July 1646 Parliament ordered that all the fortifications should be 'slighted'. Only fragments of the walls and towers now remain.*

was entrusted to Richard Bagot, formerly of Blithfield, but now deprived of his lands by Parliament. The Bagots made the new Lichfield garrison something of a family business, Richard, his brother and their parents all taking up residence and raising regiments of horse and foot to protect it. Our knowledge of how they prepared for this task is immeasurably assisted by the survival of the garrison's accounts for 1643. Here the treasurer, Jeffery Glasier, records the £10 'payde for drawing the water round about the close' and £75 'for making up the breach where the mine was sprung'. The accounts also show that the garrison was as self-sufficient as it was possible to be, cutting their own pikes, making their own beer and bread and even manufacturing gunpowder, for which they needed local supplies of saltpetre and charcoal, and sulphur imported from Sicily. Such volatile ingredients had to be milled in the close. In addition, stabling and secure pasture (between Stowe Pool and Gaia) needed to be provided for the horses. In 1643 alone the expenditure approached £9,000. The costs were met by donations from royalist sympathisers and blunt demands from others 'in His Majestie's name'.

Lichfield had now clearly nailed its colours to the King's standard, and those who supported the parliamentary cause slipped quietly away. But that cause was not long to be in the ascendancy. When King Charles spent a night in the Bishop's Palace after the Battle of Naseby in June 1645, it must have been strangely reminiscent of King Richard's hapless visit 250 years earlier. Here was another king on the long road to execution, even if he did not know it at the time. A month after the King's departure, Richard Bagot succumbed to wounds received at the battle and was buried in the south aisle of the cathedral. As the tide of the war rolled backwards it was inevitable that Lichfield close would, for a third and last time, find itself surrounded.

This final siege could not have come at a worse time, for the plague had returned to Lichfield, removing something like a third of its population. The close itself was relatively untouched, but plague and pestilence were about to replaced by another of the four apocalyptic horsemen instead. On 8 March 1646 the parliamentary forces of Sir William Brereton were in town as part of a general mopping-up operation, as the war drew towards its close. Only the royal garrisons at Oxford, Worcester and Lichfield remained to be dealt with.

On the surface the second parliamentary siege resembled that of Prince Rupert's three years earlier. The defenders withdrew to the seclusion of the close, Brereton set up his headquarters to the north of the city on Beacon Hill, while down in the city folk were still being invited to contribute to the war effort, only this time for the other side. But there were striking differences too. Those in the close were this time well supplied with stocks of food and ammunition, and Sir William had no intention of precipitously storming the walls. Instead he set about throwing a trench and bank around the area, encircling the close from Stowe Pool to Beacon Street and round to the Bishop's Fish Pool. In addition Brereton raised four 'mounts', both as vantage points for gunfire, but also to make sure that the defenders could not break out. It was as if another castle, this time of earth and wood, was being built around the one of stone.

We have Brereton's own letter-book to draw upon for an account of the progress of the third siege, giving an insight both into his military strategy and his state of mind. By the middle of April the earthworks were almost complete and the commander could consider the next stage in the assault:

Our Mortarpeeces and granadoes are also in as goode forwardnes to be played, and now am I preparing a summons to send within a day or two which I have foreborne the longer, to the end that the enemy may first bee made sensible of the improbabilitie of reliefe or of escaping; and if that receive not a satisfactory answer, to proceed to use of all means possible to reduce them otherwise.

That request to surrender was made on 13 April. The reply was short and to the point:

Though your summons has long been expected the Answer shall be shorte. Wee will keep this Garrison (God Willing) with our lives and fortunes for the King, our Liege Sovereigne by whom wee are entrusted. This is the resolution of the whole Garrison.
Your Servants,
Thomas Tyldersley
Hervey Bagot

But, short as the response was, Brereton soon had more intelligence to go on in assessing the strength of the garrison and its condition. On 28 April a soldier, William Pearson, escaped from the close and gave himself up to the enemy. His interrogation provided both good and bad news for the attackers. Food supplies in the close were still sufficient – the daily rations being half a pound of bread and half a pound of cheese or beef – but no more powder could be made and the garrison commander was on the point of turning out the horses, there being nothing left to feed them on. Pearson also revealed that the plague had at last found its way into the close: 'There is one family shut up of the sickness and a sentinel set at the door and noo person as yet dead.'

29   *Major-General Sir William Brereton, who masterminded the final decisive siege of the close in 1646. Brereton requested £6,000 from parliament for the operation, claiming that 'the Enemys strength and obstinaciousnes in the Close requires a suitable strength to be applied to reduce them'. He actually received only half this sum.*

30 *The west front of the cathedral in 1782. Though severely damaged during the three sieges of the close, much of the west front remained intact until the 1740s, when the majority of the medieval statues were removed. This engraving, therefore, is something of a fanciful reconstruction.*

Brereton's watching brief came to an end with the arrival of 60 barrels of gunpowder around 6 May. It was now the moment to make use of all those gun positions, so carefully erected over the past month. For the following six days the parliamentary gunners opened up with every piece of artillery at their disposal, from Dam Street, from the back of the *George Hotel*, and from north of Gaia Lane.

The chief target for the battery was the central spire of the cathedral. It had been used to fly royalist colours on May Day, and had always provided a more than useful vantage-point for snipers. No earthwork the attackers could raise would ever come near it. Brereton also argued that the spire was where the defenders kept their munitions, and that the royalist wives and 'grandees' were lodged there. An unlikely scenario, one suspects, but this seemingly innocent piece of masonry had undoubtedly become a very visible symbol of royalist defiance and religion and a thorn in the flesh of those who sought to change it. Remarkably, the spire survived the onslaught for five days, but on the sixth (around 11 o'clock in the morning) it came spectacularly down, crashing through the chancel roof. Brereton wrote:

Wee brought down ... this lofty proud spire which was the highest and most Comaunding of those three stately Spires which did belong to this Minster which (it is believed) were

31 *An aerial view of Lichfield cathedral close and environs in 1964. The sites of Lord Brooke's Battery, Prince Rupert's Mound and Brereton's gun positions are indicated. One estimate suggests that over 3,000 cannon balls were fired in the course of the three sieges of the close, a number of which have been recovered from the Minster Pool and close.*

erected in resemblance to the Pope's triple Crown, and if soe this downe-fall may be omen and Prognosticke of a further downefalle. The effect whereof was almost like that of Sampson's pulling down the House (with great execution) at his death.

Whatever Brereton's skills as a military tactician, he was not quite so adept at reading 'prognostickes': the pope was not about to topple, and neither was the garrison. Indeed, when next invited to capitulate, the garrison commanders this time sent a short essay of some 600 words, condemning the

32 *The cathedral choir after Victorian 'improvement'.
Bishop Hacket's restorations of the 1660s were the first
of three major reconstructions of the church. James
Wyatt removed the medieval altar screen in the 1790s, and
Samuel Smirke and George Gilbert Scott put in a metal
replacement sixty years later. Unlike the Lord himself,
ecclesiastical tastes are always changing.*

defacement of 'one of the most Auncient Monuments in this Kingdom' and vowing to be martyrs to the cause. The siege was now a month old, and it was not about to end.

In fact it would drag on for another two months, beyond the fall of Oxford (on 26 June), which spelled the end of royalist hopes, and beyond even the call by the King himself for the garrison to withdraw. Sir William Brereton was not idle in all this time, but was clearly running out of ideas. Even an attempt to force the wives of the defenders into the close (presumably as a way of reducing the garrison's food supply more quickly) failed. The garrison command left them to shiver overnight outside the walls, worried (it was claimed) that their entry would bring the plague inside.

The fall of Oxford, however, was as clear a sign as was possible that further resistance was futile. On 16 July 1646 the garrison of some 65 officers and 700 common soldiers marched out of the west gate of the close, down into Beacon Street and there surrendered their arms. While the soldiers dispersed (all, at least, except for those who had been involved in the Irish wars, who remained under arrest) the families who lived in the close returned to their battered properties. On hearing the news from Oxford and Lichfield, Parliament ordered a national day of thanksgiving for 21 July. For the city of Lichfield, at least and at last, the long civil war was over.

CHAPTER FIVE

A Society of Antiquaries

After the war comes the reckoning. The fighting that had raged in and around Lichfield for four years had inevitably taken its toll: anyone walking through the city could have seen that. The church spire of St Mary's and the tower and fabric of St Chad's were the worse for mortar fire; the market cross had been pulled down by roundheads in 1643 and most of the houses on Beacon Street had been burnt by the royalists. But it was in the close that the majority of the damage was to be seen. As surveys undertaken in 1649, 1652 and 1660 describe, the vicars' hall was 'much demolished and spoiled, not worth repairing', and the deanery and many of the prebends' houses equally 'broken and torn with granadoes'. The state of the cathedral and the bishop's palace was enough to make an episcopalian despair. The former was said to be 'exceedingly ruinated', while the palace was 'very much ruinated by the warr, much lead, iron, windscott and tymber stollen away by the souldiers'.

Nor had the cessation of hostilities marked an end of the destruction. Much lead and other materials were still being removed from the cathedral at night 'by evil persons', long after the last shot was fired, while those in charge of the close 'since the enemy left it' were clearly happy to do deals for the removal of lead and iron. And in the absence of the rightful occupants (the various bishops had been away from Lichfield for years) squatters had moved in to occupy the space. The survey of 1660, for example, describes the new tenants of one property thus:

> In the house of Mr Harrison, chancellor of the church:
> Widow Withers and her daughter
> Gunsen, his wife and son, a tobacco-pipe maker
> Mrs Royle, a widow
> Jane Birde, widow
> Ellen Gardiner with children, three in number and they bastards (widow)

Robert Allen, labourer, wife and son
Pnyon, a cobbler, wife and children

If providing shelter for the poor was part of the church's mission, then the close was doing its job admirably: a miller, two tailors and their families had taken over the palace, whilst a gardener, two weavers and a letter-carrier were now living in the deanery. Dunghills were scattered across the green and pigs rooted among the graves. The glories of medieval Lichfield had self-evidently come to an end.

33 *The statue of Charles II, now outside the south transept of the cathedral. Probably the work of Sir William Wilson, it originally stood in the central niche of the west front. The return of Charles was marked by a new royal charter (1664) and the removal of a number of Presbyterian radicals from the corporation.*

The speed with which Lichfield recovered from this low point is remarkable. Less than 40 years after this survey had been undertaken, Celia Fiennes was describing Lichfield in unexpectedly glowing terms:

The town has good houses, ye Close has ye Bishops and Deanes and prebends houses which are good; the streetes are very neate and hand-some, ye Breadth and length very well and the building handsome.

More surprising still, most of this reconstruction had taken place in the few years since King Charles II had returned to the English throne in May 1660. Restoration, as far as Lichfield was concerned, had more than one meaning.

Services were reintroduced in the cathedral from June 1660, but they may well have been chilly affairs: only the chapter house and the vestry still had a roof. Only with the arrival of Bishop John Hacket in 1661 (replacing the wonderfully named, but not so wonderfully resourceful,

34 *'Two ladies of the vale.' A drawing of 1646, showing the cathedral without its central spire. Demolished by artillery fire in May 1646, it was back in place 20 years later. Complete restoration of the building probably cost more than £15,000 but, like its sister church in Coventry, Lichfield cathedral was used to rising from the ashes.*

Accepted Frewen) did repair work advance significantly. Despite being a man of 70 years, Hacket's energetic commitment to the restoration of the cathedral was remarkable, and to say that he rebuilt it is not far short of the truth. Within four years the nave, chancel and transepts had been re-roofed, and by 1666 the west window was glazed and the central spire was once more a prominent feature of the Lichfield skyline. Work remained to be done but, when the cathedral was re-dedicated on Christmas Day 1669, it was substantially complete. All this cost huge amounts of money. There were, of course, generous benefactors, such as Catherine, wife of Sir Richard Leveson of Trentham, and the Duke of York (the future James II), who paid for the glass in the west window, but here again much was due to the enterprising John Hacket. It was achieved, as a contemporary wrote, 'by barefaced begging':

> No gentleman lodged, or scarce waited in the city, to whom he did not pay his respects by way of a visit, which ended in plausible entreaties for some assistance towards rescuing his distressed church from ruin.

Among those to whom the bishop went mitre in hand was Sir Edward Bagot of Blithfield, who was told that for £8 he could buy one of the choir stalls with his name painted above it. It must have been one of the earliest attempts at corporate sponsorship in the city. In all Bishop Hacket later claimed to have collected no less than £15,000, and to have personally donated over £5,000 towards the fabric, bells and plate. The matter of bells, however, reveals that not everything went according to plan. A peal of six bells was in the tower by 1671, but these had to be melted down soon afterwards. Perhaps bell-founding was one of those traditional crafts that had decayed for lack of practice, for in 1688 the dean and chapter were writing to Elias Ashmole for cash, showing an honesty that is both disarming (as, no doubt, it was intended to be) and remarkably modern in tone:

> The deceitfulness of the ground first making our honest bell-founder lose his casting the four biggest, to the damage of £30, and now his error in oversizing the eight bells he has cast, so far that they have swallowed up all the metal for the ten; and that requires £80 more to be added to our poor fund for the other two bells, proportionable to that bigness.

Ashmole (of whom more later) was one of the city's greatest sons and benefactors, and he was finding out (as many a charitable donor has discovered since) that every good deed necessarily leads to a request for another one.

Understandably, one imagines, Bishop Hacket had taken one look at the bishop's palace and decided that it was too far gone to merit repair. He moved into one of the neighbouring prebends' houses and spent £800 restoring this instead, probably using the ruins of the palace as a source of stone. His successor, Thomas Wood, was not so flexible, going as far as to sue the bishop's son for neglect of his lawful residence. The rebuilding of the palace did not take place until 1686, with both Bishop Wood and Sir Andrew Hacket forced to contribute a total of £3,000 towards the project. Having rebuilt the palace, however, it was found that no bishop wanted to live there, preferring Eccleshall Castle instead. For almost 200 years the house had to be rented out to various canons and vicars and, at one point, an ex-governor of Madras. Only with the appointment of George Augustus Selwyn in the late 1860s did the dean and chapter find a bishop who was willing to move in, and then only after he had added two additional wings and a chapel.

Elsewhere in the city there was also much restoration to be done, made somewhat easier by the tendency of fires to remove some of the older timbered buildings, as happened in 1681. The style was now to use brick and stone, and thatched roofs were banned by the corporation in the wake of yet another fire in 1697. Few houses from this period survive unaltered in the city today, although the Dr Johnson Birthplace Museum is clearly one, as is 20 St John Street, opposite Wade Street. In times of financial need the Conduit Lands Trust were usually on hand to provide assistance, and it was the trust which paid for a new house for the master of the grammar school in 1680. From its medieval beginnings at St John's Hospital the school had migrated across the road in 1577, effectively moving from church to corporation control. The trust purchased land from Mary Burton, the daughter of Walter Burton, musician, and then spent something like £190 constructing a place of residence for both the master and boarders.

If anything shows that investment in education pays off it is the success of the grammar school from this point onwards. Under the mastership of Robert Shaw (1680-1704) and John Hunter (1704-41) the school produced a long line of notable alumni, including five judges; the essayist, Joseph Addison; the poet, Isaac Hawkins Browne; and the inventor, John Wyatt. And even their considerable achievements are overshadowed by those of the actor, David Garrick, and the writer and lexicographer, Samuel Johnson. It should be added that such a success rate was not achieved without strong-arm tactics. Hunter's relationship with his pupils usually involved a stick, as Johnson was to recall in later life:

> He used to beat us unmercifully; and he did not distinguish between ig-norance and negligence; for he would beat a boy equally for not knowing a thing as for neglecting to know it.

Still, the Reverend Hunter's oft repeated explanation to his charges – 'This I do to save you from the gallows' – at least created a generation of men who would be able to send others there instead. Unfortunately this capital investment in education – the trust spent a further £548 on repairs to the school and house in 1768 – was never matched by increases in salary, and both the headmaster and usher found themselves taking in increasing numbers of paying pupils to meet their out-goings. Nevertheless, the grammar school in St John's Street was at least partly responsible for the extraordinary flowering of antiquarian scholarship in the city in the first half of the 18th century. No doubt there were other reasons behind it – the city's tradition as a place of learning and the parlous state of that tradition in the wake of the Commonwealth – but still it remains a considerable achievement for a city of such moderate size. Antiquarianism, as conceived in the Caroline and early Georgian period, was admittedly a strange mixture of heraldry, local history, alchemy, astrology and herbalism, but for its aspiring scholarship alone it deserves attention.

Chronologically the earliest of the group is Elias Ashmole (1617-92), 'the greatest virtuoso and curioso who was ever known or read of in England

35 *Engraving of Elias Ashmole, aged 39 years, by William Faithorne. The portrait cost Ashmole £7. The portrait incorporates Ashmole's interests in astrology, heraldry (Elias had recently discovered that his grandfather had received a grant of arms) and learning. The arched niche may refer to Ashmole's connections with freemasonry.*

before his time', who was born in Lichfield on 23 May 1617, the son of Simon Ashmole. The house believed to be his birthplace had once been the home of the guild priests and still stands in Breadmarket Street. The career of Simon Ashmole is something of a paradigm for Lichfield in this period. Born into a family tradition of saddle-making, Simon Ashmole found a career in the army in Ireland and on the Continent more appealing, and what his son called his 'ill husbandry', coupled with the general decline in the Lichfield leather industry, did not help to lift the family fortunes. But Simon's impetuous temper and immoderate ways were balanced by the qualities of his wife, Anne Bowyer. Elias calls her 'discreet, sober, provident … and excellent at her needle'.

> She was competently read in Divinity, History and Poetry, and was continually instilling into my Eares, such Religious and Moral Precepts as my younger yeares were capable off.

On the evidence of this it was his evenings at home, as much as his days at the grammar school, that set Elias on his intellectual path. The cathedral school can also claim a contribution to his upbringing, for the young Elias became a chorister there and was instructed 'on the Virginalls and Organ' by the cathedral organist. His training in vocal music came courtesy of the master of the choristers, Michael East, a well-known composer in his own right – although *Grove's Dictionary of Music and Musicians* dismisses him as 'industrious but unoriginal' – who wrote both sacred songs and anthems, as well as madrigals.

Elias Ashmole spent only the first 16 years of his life in Lichfield, before he was sent to London to study as a solicitor in the household of James Pagitt, a baron of the exchequer and a relation of his mother's. But the curious turn of Ashmole's imagination was evident long before he moved to London. The unreliable, but always intriguing, John Aubrey tells us how the young Elias made the acquaintance of a Lichfield piper who was 'entertayned by the Fayries'. The piper indicated to Ashmole the houses in the city which were 'Fayry-Ground'. Such formative influences no doubt help to explain Ashmole's somewhat bizarre range of interests and obsessions, as outlined in his journal. The diary entries flit from appointments at 'the astrologers' feast' and concerns with his collections of coins and human specimens ('dryed and preserved with spices'), to a consideration of his endless procession of illnesses (gout, toothache, boils, indigestion, constipation and ague) accompanied by their respective cures:

> This morning I grew ill, and very hot, and was troubled with sharpness of urine. I took syrup of white lilies in posset-drink, and the next day an emulsion of the four cooling seeds ... with water of violets and woodbine to wash my mouth and give myself rest and ease.

Perhaps his birthplace would now be better occupied by the Body Shop! Ashmole's subsequent career – Charles II appointed him Windsor Herald after the Restoration, as well as favouring him with a number of other lucrative posts – is beyond the scope of this book, but we must note Ashmole's lifelong interest in the affairs of his home town. He remained a generous benefactor to Lichfield at the time when the city was reconstructing itself, and included the gift of a set of services and anthems for the cathedral, and 'a large chased silver bowl and cover which cost me £23 8s. 6d.' bestowed upon the corporation in 1667. The bailiffs' overblown letter of thanks, surely commissioned from someone at the grammar school, shows that the scars from the recent war were far from healed. Lichfield is now, they write:

> ... a city that hath nothing to glory in, but its ancient and modern loyalty to God and Caesar, evidenced by her ancient Bearing in the City Escotcheon (three knights martyred), as ancient in the days of Diocletian, and her name signifying a field of blood then spilt, to which may well be added her modern and unparalleled loyalty to that blessed Saint (now in Heaven) King Charles the Martyr; universally witnessed by those honourable marks, traces and wounds of Loyalty, she yet bears upon her persons, temples, streets and walls ...

Still, Lichfield cannot regard Ashmole's influence upon the city as entirely benign, for his antiquarian researches in what remained of the cathedral library led to the removal of many manuscripts, which found their way first to his own study and then to Oxford University. The museum in Oxford which still bears his name, and was the first such institution in England, is in fact principally the collection of Ashmole's friend, John Tradescant, although the Lichfield scholar was able to supplement it with his own curiosities and papers after Tradescant's death. As Ashmole wrote characteristically in his journal on 17 February 1683: 'The last load of my rarities was sent to the barge, and this afternoon I relapsed into gout.' Appropriately, the first curator of the collection was Dr Robert Plot, another Staffordshire antiquarian. Nor was Ashmole's involvement in local politics an unalloyed pleasure. His close association with the royalist and Tory faction in the corporation led to him being approached (in 1677 and 1685) to stand as a member of parliament for the city. But Lichfield politics at this time were riven by faction, corruption and outside interference, and Elias was probably wise to have withdrawn his candidacy on both occasions, the second time on advice from King James II.

In retrospect it might look pre-ordained that a city of antiquities such as Lichfield would nurture or attract a society of antiquarians, but it was not until the late 17th and early 18th centuries that it did so. There was, it seems, something in the air in these years. A sign that such interests were spreading beyond a close circle of scholars is the appearance of Lichfield's first museum, 50 years or so after the opening of the Ashmolean. The proprietor was Richard Greene (1716-93), not himself a native of Lichfield, but one who contributed more to an appreciation of the city's history than almost anyone who was actually born there. Greene was a relation of Samuel Johnson's, an apothecary and surgeon by trade, who climbed the ladder of civic distinction to reach the office of senior bailiff. Antiquities and curiosities were very much a sideline but, for financial reasons, this was probably wise. From the 1740s onwards Greene began to build up an extensive collection of such curiosities and opened them to the public in his house on the south side of Sadler (later Market) Street.

The modern museum curator would doubtless cringe at the directionless juxtaposition of mechanical contrivances (including a remarkable clock, in the shape of a church tower, now in the Victoria Museum in Bath), artefacts from the South Seas, armour and archaeological finds, but museology was

36 *Richard Greene's museum from Stebbing Shaw's* Antiquities of
Staffordshire *(1798), showing the famous musical altar clock. The clock
jostled for space with Roman funerary urns, old tradesmen's tokens, Civil
War bullets, medieval stained glass, kidney stones and the odd foetus
(human and animal) preserved in jars.*

37 *Lichfield Museum in 1910, showing that clutter was not limited to
the 18th-century museum. The motley collection occupied an upper room
in the library building in Bird Street, before being moved to the former
probate court next door. It closed in 1970. Lichfield's failure to maintain
a fully-fledged museum is one of the more curious aspects of the place,
given its tourist potential.*

then in its infancy. What was perhaps most original about Greene's work was the attempt, almost for the first time, to preserve and commemorate the history of his adopted home. Any object of historical interest unearthed in the close tended to find its way into his museum and Greene also filled his notebooks with transcriptions and copies of important manuscripts that came his way. He it was who put up the plaque in Dam Street to mark the spot where Lord Brooke had been shot and, at Dr Johnson's request, supervised the erection of the monument to Johnson's parents and brother in St Michael's church. Sadly, however, the museum itself died with him. It was fitting, perhaps, that a collection which had been brought together from the four corners of the world was dispersed again to equally scattered locations.

A generation before Greene another Lichfield medical man had also been turning his antiquarian studies to practical use. Sir John Floyer (1649-1734), a former physician to Charles II, settled in Lichfield in the 1670s, where he set up in Colstubbe House (opposite St John's Hospital) and produced a large number of medical tracts, some of which were printed by Michael Johnson, the father of Samuel. Floyer's particular area of interest – you might almost call it an obsession – was water and its curative or restorative properties. As such he was the right man in the right place: from the time that St Chad had elected to spend some time standing in a well through to the work of the Conduit Lands trustees (of which Floyer was a prominent member) Lichfield people had found water a subject of endless fascination. In his writings Floyer argued that the custom of bathing had kept the population of Roman Britain healthy, and its discontinuation had let in many of the diseases of the modern world.

Nor was Floyer content to consign his theory to print alone. Under his energetic tutelage Lichfield became something of a spa town, not quite in the same league as Bath or Cheltenham, but locally significant nevertheless. A chalybeate spring close to St Chad's Well at Stowe was enclosed by the Conduit Lands Trust in 1695, and a small cover built over it 30 years later, and people did indeed resort to Stowe 'to drink the waters and other diversion there to take'. More ambitiously, in 1701 Floyer took out a lease on a well at Abnalls (between Lichfield and Burntwood) and built what he called St Chad's Bath. For a small fee (though Floyer stipulated that the poor should be admitted free of charge) customers could enjoy the vicarious pleasure of cold bathing. Unlike the Romans, however, the bathers at Abnalls were not allowed the compensation of mixed bathing: a brick wall separated the changing rooms.

But as with Richard Greene's museum, Sir John's particular passion did not survive him long. By the time that another Lichfield doctor, Erasmus Darwin, re-discovered the spring in the 1780s it was overgrown and abandoned. The somewhat stilted inscription he set up there, having given the site a gardening make-over, shows Darwin in unusually lyrical vein:

> If the meek flower of bashful dye,
> Attract not thy incurious eye;
> If the soft, murmuring rill, to rest
> Encharm not thy tumultuous breast,
> Go, where Ambition lures the vain,
> Or Avarice barters peace for gain.

One of the men at the centre of the antiquarian revival in the 17th-century Midlands was Sir William Dugdale (1605-86), a native of Shustoke in Warwickshire and Garter king-of-arms under Charles II. Elias Ashmole married his daughter, and another Lichfield native, Gregory King, became his clerk. There are a number of similarities between the careers of Gregory King (1648-1712) and Elias Ashmole. Both were sons of fathers who were considered profligate and intemperate, although King's father's career as a mathematician and designer of ornamental gardens and sun-dials was probably even more precarious than that of a saddler. Both sons attended the grammar school, though again Gregory's mastery of Latin, Greek and Hebrew suggests outside interference. As clerk to William Dugdale, Gregory King accompanied him on visitations across the country in the 1660s, after which King supported himself by teaching writing and arithmetic and pandering to the new interest in genealogy back in his native city. King was teaching in Lichfield in 1669, but much of his later life was based in London, where he designed the lay-out of new streets in Soho Fields. Soho Square was initially known as King's Square in recognition of his efforts. Like Ashmole too, King had a boundless curiosity for the oddities of life, as his surviving notebook often reveals:

28 June 1679. Came up to Town by Bass the Carrier of Tamworth a Child of 3 year old born at Manchester, who they pretend can speak Latin Greek & Hebrew and has 3 words to say to the King after which it will live but 9 days. Supposed to speak like a parrot, more, only.

But it is as a statistician that Gregory King deserves particular notice, an art still very much in its infancy at this time. King's work entitled *Natural* and *Political Observations and Conclusions upon the State and Condition of England*, written in 1696, is the best attempt to estimate the population of England at the close of the 17th century. Gregory King's breakthrough was to combine his undoubted skills as a mathematician with his geographical knowledge, extrapolating national totals of population from local taxation returns. His one-man census of Lichfield, undertaken in 1695, gives us our first reliable figure for the total population of the city: he counted 205 people living in the close and 2,833 in the town.

The examples of Elias Ashmole and Gregory King show that the battered and bruised city of Lichfield was still capable of producing individuals of powerful and original intellect, even if it was not quite so adept at keeping them there. Then, as now, it was necessary to take the high road to London to build a reputation and an income. And if this was true of antiquarians, it was even more so of writers and artists, and it is to this group that we must now turn.

Dean Lancelot Addison (1632-1703) was not a name to be remembered with a great deal of affection in the cathedral close. One biographer calls him 'impetuous, tactless and warmhearted' and his spats both with the bishop and the chapter undoubtedly disrupted the smooth running of the diocese during the 1680s and 1690s. Political change, however, undermined him and probably ruined his chance of a bishopric. Addison was a Tory and a traditionalist, a fierce opponent of puritanism (as well as of Islam), and the Glorious Revolution of 1688, which replaced James II with William of Orange, did him no favours. Addison was no glorious revolutionary. Little wonder that it was 15 years after his death before a monument to the troublesome dean was erected on the west wall of the cathedral.

Yet Dean Addison's name is worth recalling if only for the achievements of his son, who could hardly have been more removed from his father in political sentiments. Joseph Addison (1672-1719) was a boy of 11 years when his father was translated to Lichfield. The move from Wiltshire to Staffordshire at least allowed Addison junior to avail himself of the excellent educational opportunities open to him at the grammar school. Under Robert Shaw the young Joseph acquired that firm grounding in the classics which society demanded of its élite. Indeed, so sure was this cultural foundation that Addison not only knew Latin poetry back-to-front, but composed it himself. His Latin poems on such varied subjects as a bowling green, a puppet show and a barometer attracted high praise from, amongst others, Macaulay. Not all of

Joseph's school days, however, were spent on such cerebral pursuits: Samuel Johnson, who followed Addison to the same school a few years later, tells us that his predecessor led a riot against an unpopular teacher there. The standard of pupil behaviour has clearly not declined over the centuries!

Addison's sojourn in Lichfield was brief. In 1686 he was sent to Charterhouse school in London, thence to Oxford, the Grand Tour and the big wide world of politics and literature. There was one brief return to the city in 1718 to supervise the erection of his father's monument in the cathedral, but the rest of Addison's life was spent in the London coffee-houses and at his desk. In addition to poetry and plays he churned out a staggering number of articles first for the *Tatler*, then the *Spectator* and then the *Guardian*; indeed, in many instances he wrote the whole issue. Perhaps the grammar school and the deanery can claim more than a little influence on that classical elegance of style and breadth of learning evident throughout his work, even if his whiggish sympathies were decidedly at odds with both places.

It would seem that a biographical pattern is beginning to emerge in this procession of famous men: impecunious and impetuous fathers, devoted but fragile mothers and brilliant sons. Perhaps their respective biographers have followed the social stereotype rather too slavishly. That said, the same blueprint emerges once more with David Garrick (1717-79), who rose from humble origins to become the leading actor of Georgian England, and arguably the most famous actor-manager of them all.

Garrick's Lichfield connections were considerably more substantial than those of the men we have already discussed. His mother, Arabella Clough, was herself a native of the city, the daughter of one of the vicars choral, and it was here that she met Peter Garrick, who was then an ensign in a foot regiment. Peter Garrick's army career took him far and wide: to Hereford, where David was born, and then to Gibraltar. As a result, David Garrick saw little of his father until 1736, though he saw a great deal more of Lichfield. The family home was in Beacon Street but, unlike the more substantial houses of Ashmole and Darwin, it no longer survives. A plaque on the wall of the probate court building marks its location. Arabella's efforts to raise seven children – the oldest, Peter, left home early to become a midshipman in the West Indies – took its toll on her health and David Garrick helped to shoulder the family burden. But as Garrick's schooling progressed, his career as an actor-manager was already under way. In 1728 or 1729 he directed a production of George Farquhar's *The Recruiting Sergeant* on a makeshift stage in the bishop's palace, with himself in the role of Kite. Farquhar's work was understandably popular in Lichfield; the dramatist had lodged at the *George* in Bird Street, whilst he was both acting as a recruiting sergeant and writing a play on the same theme. George Farquhar's last play, *The Beaux' Stratagem*, first performed at the Queen's Theatre, Haymarket, six weeks before he died, is actually set in the city.

Once Garrick's father had returned from Gibraltar he had two of his sons enrolled in a new academy at Edial Hall, just outside the city. The school promised much. It was a private and potentially exclusive establishment; the hall itself was impressively modern and set in its own grounds; and the proprietor had a growing local reputation as a scholar. Sadly for the Garricks and the proprietor, who happened to be Samuel Johnson, an educated man does not necessarily make a good educator. Due chiefly to Johnson's eccentricities and wayward behaviour, Edial Hall was a disaster and had closed within a year. It did, however, serve to bring together the scholar and the actor. It was not a relationship that always ran smoothly and Garrick's rise to wealth and status did not endear him to the perennially penurious Johnson. (Had Johnson ever seen Garrick's uproarious take-off of the schoolmaster in matrimonial mood, learnt through key-hole observations at

Edial and performed as a party-piece for his friends, he would have been even less forgiving.) But with Garrick unable to afford to go to university, and Johnson unable to make it as a teacher, the two men set out together for London (where fortunes were made) on 2 March 1737.

Within four years David Garrick was the talk of the London stage. To say that the actor was lucky in choosing to specialise in Shakespeare, just as the dramatist was due for a comeback, is probably to underestimate Garrick's own role in that revival. Had there been no Garrick, there would have been no Shakespeare Jubilee in 1769, and one

38 *David Garrick as King Lear, in an engraving based on the painting by Benjamin Wilson. Garrick first played the part in 1770 at the age of 53, and the artist, Joshua Reynolds, was so moved by the performance that it took him three days to recover. The version performed by Garrick had a happy ending, a refinement that Addison condemned as removing half the play's beauty.*

wonders at what stage England's greatest playwright would have risen to his present preeminence. In the short term, for Garrick at least, it was a lucrative move. As he wrote to his brother, Peter, back in Lichfield in October 1741:

> Last night I played Richard the Third to the surprise of everybody, and as I shall make near £300 per annum by it, and it is really what I dote upon, I am resolved to pursue it.

Peter himself would have been somewhat surprised by this revelation. He thought that his brother was working as a wine merchant! Both Peter and David Garrick recognised that putting a son on the stage was not going to improve the family's social standing in Lichfield, and they were probably right. But David was no average player, and the fame that came his way was appreciated locally, as celebrity is anywhere and in any sphere. By 1742 Lichfield was organising coach parties to go and see their famous prodigy:

39 *The David Garrick theatre in Bore Street, representing Lichfield's brief return in the 1950s to its theatrical tradition. The second producer at the ill-fated theatre was Kenneth Tynan, who directed a production of* The Beaux' Stratagem. *Occupying the site of the city's first playhouse, it survived for only four years. The building was demolished in 1992. Garrick's name is now commemorated in the newly expanded civic hall.*

> The night before last I saw Mr Sudall, who with more Lichfield people came to see *The Rehearsal*. I have the greatest success imaginable in the part of Bayes, and instead of clapping me they huzza, which is very uncommon approbation …

A full account of David Garrick's career is beyond the scope of this book, particularly as it bears little upon Lichfield. Garrick could hardly forget what

40 *The survival of so many of Lichfield's shopfronts helps to give the town a sense of commercial continuity. Charrington's shop in Market Street (photographed here in 1952) stood at the end of a tradition that reached back to Richard Greene and beyond. In 1793 there were four apothecaries operating in Lichfield.*

he called his native place ('though dropped at Hereford'), since his family continued to live there, but there were usually more substantial dinner tables to eat at than the one in Beacon Street. It is worth noting, however, that in 1754, when Garrick and his wife moved into Fuller House, their palatial new residence beside the Thames, he recruited staff from Lichfield to run it. Suffice to say that on his death in January 1779 Garrick became the second of Lichfield's sons (after Addison) to find his final resting-place in Westminster Abbey. It was certainly a star-studded funeral: Richard Sheridan was the chief mourner and Edmund Burke was heard to sob as the coffin was lowered into the abbey floor. But let Sam Johnson, who also shed a tear, deliver the final eulogy. The doctor's epitaph for his erstwhile companion shows that mixture of puzzlement, admiration and superciliousness that we would expect of an academic confronting popular culture:

I am disappointed by that stroke of death, which has eclipsed the gaiety of nations, and impoverished the public stock of harmless pleasure.

Which brings us, of course, to the great man himself.

CHAPTER SIX

A City of Philosophers

Those who call at Lichfield market today and raise their eyes above the cakes and the carrots will see that Dr Samuel Johnson (1709-84) continues to be a brooding presence in the city of his birth. The portentous statue erected in the market square in 1838 (by Richard Cockle Lucas) proves as much. Johnson's salute to his home town in his famous dictionary – 'Salve magne parens' – has even been incorporated into the city's armorial bearings. Indeed, the good doctor occupies such an eminent place in the history and culture of Lichfield that it seems almost superfluous to add anything. But times and taste have changed and the achievements and attractions of a Georgian writer and conversationalist are no longer quite so easy to grasp. Today Johnson would have a TV chat show and a regular newspaper column to demonstrate his talents. No such platform was possible in the 18th century. What Johnson showed the literary establishment, as Shakespeare before

41 Richard Lucas's statue of Dr Johnson in the market place, here the centrepiece of the birthday celebrations in December 1950. A statue of the doctor's friend and biographer, James Boswell, was unveiled nearby in 1908. The contrast between the slight and rather effete Boswell and his pondering and ponderous companion could hardly be more pronounced.

42   *Dr Johnson's birthplace in the 1830s. At this date the building was the office of the* Lichfield Mercury, *the city's first (weekly) newspaper, which transferred from Stafford in 1815. It was a brief occupation. The paper folded in 1833, although the title was later revived. At various times in the 19th century there was also a* Lichfield Advertiser, Chronicle, Mercury *and* Herald.

him, was that it was possible, indeed more likely, that talent and aspiration came from the provinces, and although London might suck in the artists (such as Ashmole and King and Addison and Garrick) it could never entirely expunge their regional origins. For our purposes, however, Johnson's fame and his loquacious pen have served to open up Lichfield society to our eyes to an extent impossible for any other provincial town of the period.

Samuel Johnson's father, Michael Johnson, had settled in Lichfield in 1681 to trade as a bookseller, printer and bookbinder in Sadler Street. As such he relied heavily upon customers from the close, where reading was almost as common a pastime as gossiping. But his customer base in the environs of the cathedral would never be as broad as in, say, York or Lincoln, and Johnson senior supplemented work in his shop with peripatetic bookselling in the markets of Uttoxeter, Trentham and Birmingham. Samuel's memory was of a family always on the brink of financial ruin:

> The truth was, that my father, having in the early part of his life contracted debts, never had trade sufficient to enable him pay them, and maintain his family; he got something, but not enough.

Financial uncertainty was not exactly compatible with Johnson's social, domestic and commercial ambitions, but he pursued them nonetheless. Having married Sarah Ford, the daughter of a prosperous Birmingham family, Michael Johnson built a new house in Breadmarket Street, fronting onto Lichfield market, to serve both as a shop and a family home, although its size (with no fewer than 11 bedrooms and two kitchens) was probably far in excess of the potential size of his family or his business. Sarah was already 37 years old and her husband 12 years older still. No doubt Johnson's decision to open what he called a 'parchment factory' beside Stowe Pool was also a perfectly laudable attempt to control his expenses, but it was never a commercial success. In later life Samuel recalled how his father habitually locked the front gate to the factory long after it was a simple matter to walk through the ruins of the back of the shop. At the time it convinced him that his father was on the verge of a breakdown. The birth of a son in 1709 coincided with Michael's election as sheriff, and the banquet thrown that year at the Ridings was especially lavish. This would not have helped the bookseller's finances.

A number of people can take credit for the survival of this sickly child: the celebrated local physician, George Hector, who acted in the unusual role of 'man-midwife'; the wife of a local brickmaker who nursed him; Dr Swinfen, who diagnosed that the young child had contracted scrofula, and (less plausibly) Dr Floyer, who advised that Samuel be taken to London to be 'touched' by the Queen. The tradition of the sovereign touching for the disease known as 'the King's Evil' had recently been revived – James II had once performed the ceremony in Lichfield cathedral – and it was typical of Dr Floyer to mix his medicine, his theology and his royalism in such a manner. The cure was, of course, singularly unsuccessful, but did provide the three-year-old infant with his first glimpse of the metropolis where he would spend most of his life. Johnson himself recollected little of the occasion beyond 'some confused remembrances of a lady in diamonds and a long black hood'. This, we may assume, was Queen Anne.

Samuel Johnson was to spend the first 28 years of his life in and around Lichfield, until that day in March 1737 when he set out for London with his friend, David Garrick. Such was the fame (though not so much of the fortune) that came to him later that Lichfield and his many biographers have endeavoured to preserve as much as possible of his early associations with the city. The birthplace itself was sold on Samuel's death for £235, but a century later came into the ownership of the city council for almost the same amount. It was opened to the public in 1901 as one of the first museums in the country to be devoted to a single individual. Johnson's earliest biographer, William Shaw, understandably attributes his encyclopaedic knowledge of poetry and the classics to 'lounging here', and living over a bookshop could hardly have failed to direct his steps towards a literary life.

As for Samuel's formal education there is decidedly less to see today. The dame school on the corner of Dam Street and Quoniams Lane, run by Ann

43 *Quoniams Lane, showing the site (and possibly the place) of Samuel Johnson's first school. Much of the street is now occupied by Linford Bridgeman Ltd. The founder of the famous firm, Robert Bridgeman, came to Lichfield to work on the restoration of the west front of the cathedral in 1878. His work in the city includes the statue of Edward VII in Museum Gardens and the war memorial beside Minster Pool.*

Oliver, where he learnt the rudiments of reading and writing, was substantially rebuilt in the late 18th or early 19th century, though some earlier timbers are preserved inside. The grammar school building in St John Street, where Johnson's learning was already a subject of admiration among his fellows, has also gone, leaving only the newly-built master's house, which John Hunter shared with his more lucrative boarders. Their names, though not their cries for help, are preserved in the graffiti on the attic rafters.

The area around Stowe Pool has many Johnson associations, provided one has the imagination to reconstruct them. Here the young Samuel once accidentally stepped on a duckling and was prompted by his father to compose an epitaph for the unfortunate creature which begins: 'Here lies poor duck, which Samuel Johnson trod on …'. Here too Samuel learnt to swim, and wrote a Latin poem to fix this poignant memory. In translation it reads:

Clear as glass the stream still meanders through the green fields.
Here, as a boy, I bathed my tender limbs,
Unskilled, frustrated, while with gentle voice
My father from the bank taught me to swim.

Here too he took a scientific interest in a willow tree that grew near his father's parchment works. The willow now standing is at least the fourth in line from the one described to Johnson in 1781 as being 'near fourscore years, and some respectable authorities strongly incline to think a century has passed over its head'. With a height of 49 feet and a trunk 15 feet in circumference, the tree was remarkable enough even without its literary associations.

In the period between 1770 and the end of the century the city authorities were especially active in landscaping the surrounds of both Minster and Stowe Pools, laying out walks and planting islands. It was this work that twisted the rectangle of the Minster Pool into the serpentine shape still seen today. Such changes are well preserved in John Snape's map of the city of 1781, showing the 'New Walk' on the south side of Minster Pool and Parchment House on the site of Michael Johnson's factory to the north of Stowe Pool. It was at exactly this time that John Saville, one of the vicars choral, was turning part of the grounds into a famous botanical and flower garden, beloved of Erasmus Darwin and Anna Seward, who was also (to the horror of the close) rather fond of Mr Saville himself, despite his married status. Stebbing Shaw reports that the garden contained 'above 700 specimens of rare and elegant plants, well worthy of the notice of the curious'. Snape's map also serves to remind us that Stowe Pool was less than half the length we can see today, the stretch near to Johnson's willow, where the clothmakers had their tenters, being marshy ground known as 'Stowe Moggs'. As they had done for centuries past, tan yards continued to surround and infringe the marsh and the stream which led to the Dam Street mill. The third of the city's pools, west of Bird Street, had also silted up by this date, and had to relinquish its grand old name of 'the Bishop's Fish Pool' for the more prosaic 'Swan Moggs'. The bishop was more likely to find frogs there than fish.

The city's churches too maintain their Johnsonian connections. St Michael's contains Johnson's inscriptions to his father, mother and brother, Nathaniel, in which the formality of the Latin gives way to more personal affection. The arrangements were handled by Richard Greene, the apothecary and museum curator. Johnson wrote to him in December 1794:

The first care must be to find the exact place of interment, that the stone may protect the bodies. Then let the stone be deep, massy and hard; and do not let the difference of ten pounds, or more, defeat our purpose.

The stone was laid a matter of weeks before Samuel's own death. The Johnson family church, St Mary's, did not have an external burial ground and so they were laid to rest at Greenhill. The parish registers of St Michael's, perused by Stebbing Shaw, show that burials exceeded christenings there throughout the final quarter of the century for exactly this reason.

The family's servant, Kitty Chambers, is commemorated by a plaque in St Chad's. Samuel was present at her death in October 1767, writing movingly in his diary:

Yesterday … at about ten in the morning I took leave for ever of my dear old friend Catherine Chambers, who came to live with my mother about 1724, and has been little parted from us since … She told me that to part was the greatest pain she had ever felt, and that she hoped we should meet again in a better place. I expressed with swelled eyes and great emotion of tenderness the same hopes.

Lucy Porter, Johnson's step-daughter by his wife's previous marriage, whom he described as having 'lost the beauty and gaiety of youth, without having gained much of the wisdom of age', is also buried here.

But of all the connections, perhaps the most extraordinary was that of Francis Barber, Johnson's servant and the chief beneficiary of his will. Barber was a former slave from Jamaica, who came to live in Johnson's house in Gough Square a few weeks after his wife's death. Give or take the occasional disappearance, Barber remained by Johnson's side for the rest of his life. On Johnson's death Barber moved to Lichfield, where he married a local girl and lived in Stowe Street. When the money ran out, like his master before him, Frank Barber opened a small school – probably a dame school – in Burntwood, but like Edial it was not a success and had closed by 1799. Barber himself died in 1801. No doubt he was not the first black person to live in Lichfield, but perhaps among the earliest.

For Johnson himself, however, there were greater glories than mere burial: a funeral in Westminster Abbey and an enduring literary legacy. The latter was not quick to arrive; there was a spell working as a journalist in Birmingham, the abortive attempt to set up as a schoolmaster, and then the flood of articles, translations and a play, *Irene*, which Garrick staged (12 years after it was written) in 1749. Only with the appearance of *A Dictionary of the English Language* in 1755 did he belatedly enter the pantheon of great scholars, a work which exemplifies both his linguistic sensitivity and his vast knowledge of the corpus of English literature. In an age of databases and search engines it is easy to underestimate what a heroic task this was. There followed from its publication an honorary degree from Oxford University (Johnson had been forced by lack of money to leave Oxford without one), a doctorate from Trinity College, Dublin, and a life pension of £300 from the king. But it was as an essayist that Samuel Johnson was at his best, a skill best shown in his prefaces to the plays of Shakespeare (which he also edited) and by the monumental ten volumes of his *Lives of the Most Eminent English Poets* (1779-81).

Inevitably much of the great man's life was spent in the capital, but (unlike Garrick) his travels often took him

44 *A copy of Joshua Reynolds' famous portrait of Johnson. William Shaw wrote of Johnson: 'His mind was as destitute of accommodation as his exterior was of politeness or grace; and to those who estimate genius or worth only by a soft tongue, a smooth face or ceremonious carriage, his wit would appear insolence, his honesty folly, and his learning pedantry.'*

back to his home town, even if he was not (to his eternal regret) in time to visit his mother on her death-bed. From the late 1760s Johnson usually made an annual pilgrimage back to the Midlands, a trip which always included Ashbourne (where a former school friend, John Taylor, lived) and Lichfield. He usually stayed at the *Three Crowns* in Breadmarket Street, only yards from the house where he was born. Such a regular journey would not have been impossible a century earlier, but it would certainly have been more arduous, especially for a man in his sixties.

Without much of an industrial tradition to rely on, transport and communications were the life-blood of the city. Johnson might well say to

45 *Edial Hall near Burntwood in 1824, where 'young gentlemen are boarded and taught the Latin and Greek languages by Samuel Johnson' as the advertisement ran. The hall itself was later demolished, leaving only the 18th-century farmhouse (to the left of the engraving), which had once housed servants from the hall.*

Boswell that Lichfield was 'a city of philosophers; we work with our heads, and make the boobies of Birmingham work for us with their hands', but such a division of labour was not good news to the small traders and manufacturers of his home town. Luckily for them the roads which for centuries had entered or passed near Lichfield saved it from complete isolation. Given their age they were in remarkably good condition. Robert Plot and John Ogilby had no particular cause for complaint and neither did Celia Fiennes, passing through in the 1690s:

> From hence we went to Litchfield 7 mile, a sandy Road full of fine pebbles; Litchfield stands Low, there is a greate standing water as I have seen just by ye town, which does often flow ye grounds after Raines, so the Road is secured with a banck and a breast wall of a good length into ye town …

Nevertheless, the areas to the north and south of Lichfield – the Potteries and the Black Country – were industrialising fast, and the roads would soon be deteriorating accordingly from the increase in heavy traffic. Upkeep of roads and bridges was a parish responsibility, but it was rarely a duty that the churchwardens had at the top of their list of priorities. Thus we read in 1662 that Yoxall Bridge, carrying the road from Lichfield to Kings Bromley, was:

> ... in peril of great decay and the groundwork founderous, and will cost threescore and ten pounds to repair, and if speedy reparacon be not made, the same will be utterly ruined.

Lichfield was an important post town on the route from London to Ireland from the 1570s and had a local service, delivered on foot, by the 1680s, but this only served to highlight the problem of poor maintenance. In 1674 the deputy postmaster general had cause to complain to the Lichfield postmaster that: 'Your riders are oftener lost in the night, and have more unfortunate accidents happen to them on your roads than halfe England besides.'

The national solution to this situation, applied locally, was the turnpike, and after the arrival of the first toll road in Staffordshire in 1714 a series of petitions found their way (bumpily, no doubt) to Westminster, decrying the state of the highways and seeking redress by what amounted to privatisation. Given the profits that might accrue, we ought probably to take these complaints with a pinch of salt, but we cannot ignore them. In 1728 a petition to the House of Commons from the inhabitants of Stone and Lichfield sought leave to introduce a bill to turnpike three routes: the London to Chester road from Cannal's Gate to Lichfield and Stone; the Burton to Birmingham road from Burton-on-Trent to Lichfield and Shenstone; and the Uttoxeter road from Lichfield to Tewnhall's Lane and High Bridges. The third of these was described as 'impassable in winter', the condition of the second was dismissed as 'very bad', whilst of the first the postmaster of Stone gave evidence that:

> ... it was worn deep with heavy carriages, and although large sums of money have been laid out by contributors and the statute labour constantly done, yet that has not been sufficient to keep the same in repair, and when any quantity of snow falls many coaches have left the road, and post boys with packets have been unable to pass.

The act was passed in 1728, effectively turnpiking all the major thoroughfares into the city, with the exception of the Tamworth road, which was not turnpiked until 1770. The same act set up the Lichfield Turnpike Trust to administer the system and we can see familiar names such as Sir John Floyer, Samuel Swinfen and Gilbert Walmesley among the trustees.

The theory of the turnpike was that travellers would now be charged to use the roads and these funds (once an honest profit had been taken) would be directed towards road improvements. A typical charge was sixpence for a coach and ten pence for a herd of cattle, though much agricultural traffic was specifically exempted. Tickets were issued at the turnpike gates, which from the passing of the first act began to ring the city. One tollhouse stood at the junction of Beacon Street and Wheel Lane, another beside St John's Hospital and another at the bottom of Tamworth Street. By the date of John Snape's plan (1781) there were seven such gates. It must have seemed as if the medieval boundaries of the city (not to mention the bishop's market tolls) were being re-introduced. The streets within the city were outside the jurisdiction of the act, albeit that there was an implicit expectation that the civic authorities would enact comparable improvements. The Conduit Lands Trust did indeed widen the bridge on Bird Street in 1760 (to about four metres), but the approach to the bridge along St John Street still remained inconveniently narrow.

As long-distance traffic became heavier and communication between the major cities increased Lichfield grew in popularity as a stopping-off point, and the inns which had fed and watered travellers from medieval times enjoyed a boom. The most vivid impression of such comings and goings is the first scene of George Farquhar's play, *The Beaux' Stratagem*, set in the *George Inn*. While the travellers from the Warrington coach wait impatiently in the hotel lobby, they are joined by another coach-load from London, ready to be directed to various inns in the city. Lichfield residents must have been used to the arrival of such coach parties, and organised their drinking parties accordingly.

Coaches plying the road between London and Chester were calling at Lichfield from the 1650s, and Dugdale took this route to the capital in the 1660s, probably on the carrier service run by the junior bailiff, James Rixam. This was certainly not a day trip. The Birmingham & Lichfield Stage-Coach, which delivered travellers to the capital in the 1740s, set out on Monday morning in the winter and arrived in London on Wednesday night. One hopes that the summer journey would have been somewhat shorter. Such a trip was not cheap: customers paid 37 shillings, with an allowance of 14 pounds of luggage. Additional weight, or expensive items, which might attract the unwanted attention of foot-pads or 'gentlemen of the road', incurred an additional tariff. The proprietor of this service was Anthony Jackson, landlord of the *Coach and Horses*. There were also both quicker and slower ways of making the same journey. The Lichfield Flying Wagon (an ironic name, if ever there was one) could deliver the traveller, a little older and wiser, to London in four and a half days, whilst a seat on the Royal Mail would get there far more swiftly, if at a higher price. By the 1830s this could be done in a day.

By the late 18th century Lichfield residents could have watched a procession of coaches rattling into their city. London-Chester and London-Liverpool coaches called daily, whilst others from Birmingham to Sheffield, Manchester and Derby were almost as regular. Services were advertised in the newspapers and trade directories, but in the absence of other marketing the names of the coaches made grandiose claims for their velocity: the *Quicksilver* (to Shrewsbury), the *True Blue Alert* (to Rugeley) and the *Rapid* (to Derby). The *Staffordshire General & Commercial Directory* of 1818 lists four daily coaches from Lichfield to London. None of these services, it has to be said, could compete with the horse-power of the railways, which arrived in the 1830s and killed the coach business almost overnight.

Four of the Lichfield inns cornered the market in the coaching trade. The *George*, the *Swan* (previously the *Lily White Swan*), the *King's Head* (formerly the *Antelope*) and the *Talbot* were all on Bird Street, along which the majority of the traffic passed. The *George*, the *King's Head* and the *Swan* were all medieval inns, converted in the 18th century to take advantage of the extra trade, while the *Talbot* (on the corner of Bore Street) was converted to hotel use in the 1760s. Unlike the other three the *Talbot*, it seems, catered exclusively for 'gentlemen on horseback'.

Such inns or hotels (the more up-market name was being used by the end of the 18th century) fulfilled a number of roles. Passengers might use them to wait for a connecting service or to stay overnight, while the extensive stabling at the rear (the *George* had space for 54 horses) allowed the coach to change horses. But they all had equally important roles to play in the social life of the city, and their assembly rooms were in constant use for musical functions or the annual dinners for guilds. The Cecilian Society met for an annual concert and dinner (on St Cecilia's Day, of course) at the *King's Head* from 1752, and a gentlemen's drinking club known as the 'Court of Truth' pursued their hobby at the *George* in the 1740s. Competition between these establishments was keen, in the case of the *George* and *Swan* intensified by conflicting political affiliations. The *George* was the meeting-place and headquarters of the Whig party at election time, while the Tories met in the *Swan*. Bird Street was never short of activity.

What Lichfield could undoubtedly offer the weary traveller was good ale. The city's reputation for its beer was far-flung, as Aimwell tells the landlord of the *George* in Farquhar's play. The landlord himself describes his brew as 'smooth as oil, sweet as milk, clear as amber and strong as brandy': Lichfield's age-old concern over its water supply had clearly not been wasted. The reputation of Lichfeldians for over-indulgence was also widespread: Gregory King said they were 'addicted to drinking'. As far as Dr Johnson was concerned (admittedly a man who claimed never to have been drunk in his life) this rarely did them any harm. The ale that they copiously imbibed was usually brewed on the premises; Boswell, staying at the *Three Crowns* in Breadmarket Street in 1776, sampled oat ale, as well as Staffordshire oat cakes 'not hard as in Scotland, but soft like a Yorkshire cake and served at breakfast'. He remarks rather cattily that he found it pleasant that the 'food of horses' was so much used as the food of the people in Johnson's home town. Boswell was used to defending the diet of his Scottish countrymen against Johnson's barbed comments.

However, the tradition of home-brewing was not as common as it once was and the number of maltsters and brewers supplying other establishments was growing by the end of the 18th century. The 1818 *Directory* lists 18 maltsters scattered through the town, but predominantly along Tamworth Street. The alcohol trade was one of Lichfield's major industries. The same source lists no less than 54 inns or taverns, seven of which were in Bird Street and a further five in Bore Street. And that number, believe it or not, was in decline. By the 1730s there were 80 taverns or beerhouses in Lichfield for an estimated population of around 3,500, and no fewer than 15 in St John Street alone. It was no wonder that the Hospital had a drink problem. Victorian regulation of licences would later decimate this figure. There are now only around twenty-five such premises still trading.

One customer the local publicans might not have wanted to see too often was Erasmus Darwin. Writing to the Duke of Devonshire in November 1783 Darwin asks:

> Give a man unused to vinous fluids a bottle of port or 3 pints of ale – what is the consequence? He looses his understanding, and becomes for a time an Ideot: and falling down on the floor without the use of his limbs, has a temporary paralysis! From both which he recovers by slow degrees, is left stupid and much debilitated in body for several days.

The Duke's particular complaint was gout, and Darwin had his own Lichfield experience to draw upon when advising him:

> About 7 or 8 years ago, I had three fits of Gout in three successive years; and gradually left off drinking ale and wine; and at length small beer also; and have since had not the least attack of Gout.

Such views would not have gone down well in Bird Street, for without its service industries the Lichfield economy was decidedly threadbare. Some of the earliest trade directories do not even include the place, and the lack of much commercial activity was noticed by James Boswell, when he visited the city in Johnson's company in 1776:

> Very little business seemed to be going forward in Lichfield. I found, however, two strange manufactures for so inland a place, sail-cloth and streamers for ships; and I observed them making saddle-cloths and dress-ing sheep-skins; but on the whole the busy hand of industry seemed to be quite slackened. 'Surely Sir', said I, 'you are an idle set of people.'

The sail-cloth merchant was probably John Tunstall, who had a factory at the west end of Sandford Street, while the saddlecloth and tammy (a kind of worsted) that Boswell saw may well have been made by John Hartwell, who had tenters on Stowe Moggs.

The spinning and dyeing of cloth was a medieval legacy, which, despite the corporation's resistance, hung on in Sandford Street and Stowe. A related trade – ropemaking – is also evident from Snape's map on the south side of Stowe Moggs and on Lombard Street. Leather work, once the dominant trade in the city, also survived around Sandford Street and Stowe Pool, but this profession too was under pressure from the authorities because of its pollution of the pools. That said, it was under even more pressure from the rise of Walsall as a saddlery centre. Here was certainly a lost opportunity, for Lichfield's position as a coaching town recommended it for such anciliary work. After all, 18th-century Lichfield boasted – in Erasmus Darwin and Richard Edgeworth – two residents who were connoisseurs of the carriage craft. One local carriage-maker, James Butler, did submit a patent in 1773 for a revolutionary new design, a forerunner of suspension. The spokes of the wheels were replaced by springs, so that the carriage rolled over any obstacle without jolting the occupants. But Butler's idea (probably borrowed from Darwin) did not go forward into production. There were two

46 *The market square in 1783, showing Dr Johnson's birthplace, St Mary's church and the market hall. This version of the market hall, occupying the site of the current market, stood from the 1730s to the 1790s. The hall was paid for by the Conduit Lands Trust: all the corporation had to supply was the bell.*

coachmakers in the city in the 1770s, but exactly the same number (appropriately in Bird Street and St John Street) operating in 1818.

Attempts to kick-start the metal industry in Lichfield were also singularly unsuccessful. Stowe Mill had been converted to iron by the 1740s, but was back milling flour a decade or so later. Even more revealing than Boswell's and Johnson's discussion of the city's lack of industry is their meeting with an old school-friend of the doctor's. This man had gone to Birmingham to seek his fortune as a cutler, but by 1776 was back in Lichfield, considering a career in ornamental leather. It was quite clear, even without Johnson's pronouncement, that Lichfield had quite intentionally crossed the manufacturing divide and become a consumer rather than a producer. If that situation implied to Johnson some kind of post-industrial superiority, he was not the only one to remark upon it. A contemporary German visitor, Carl Philip Moritz, in the course of dismissing Lichfield's urban landscape as 'narrow, dirty and unfriendly', admitted that his opinion had partly been coloured by the remarks of the daughter of a Sutton landlord, who had told him that Lichfeldians thought too much of themselves.

Still, as Lichfield's leisured classes grew, so too did the trade in consumer durables. Michael Johnson's bookselling business might have been parlous, but it stubbornly refused to fold. It was carried on successively by his son, his widow and their servant and then by another bookseller, Major Morgan, who continued to trade into the 1800s. Anna Seward is our best witness for all this consumerism. She speaks of hairdressers running about the city all morning as Lichfield grew 'more fine and fashionable every day', and there were indeed seven such beauticians operating in the city in 1818. The Lichfield shops at the close of the 18th century reflect a clientèle with considerable disposable income: milliners, tea-dealers, musical instrument makers, watchmakers and confectioners, to name but a few of the more common traders. That said, Miss Seward still found shopping in Bath or London more exciting.

Lichfield is blessed with the survival of a handful of shop-fronts from this period, the best of which stands next to the *George Hotel* in Market Street (and incorporates part of the carriageway entrance with its original Rowley Ragstone paving). The shop-front of 3 Market Street dates from around 1780, and was a leather-maker's workshop, as were a number of businesses in the street.

47 *The statue of James Boswell in the market place, at its unveiling in 1908. Boswell visited Lichfield in 1776 with his mentor. In his* Life of Johnson *Boswell wrote: 'I felt all my old Toryism glowing in this old capital of Staffordshire. I could have offered incense to the genius of the place; and indulged in libations of that ale, which Boniface, in* The Beaux' Stratagem, *recommends with such an eloquent jollity.'*

48   *Dr Johnson's statue and birthplace in the market place. One door away from Johnson's house in Breadmarket Street is the* Three Crowns *public house, where Johnson often stayed on his visits to Lichfield. In the late 18th century the inn hosted an early freemasons' lodge, probably chosen because of its proximity to the birthplace of Elias Ashmole, a famous member of the order.*

The twice-weekly market, however, remained the hub of Lichfield's commercial traffic. It will be remembered that Bishop Denton's old market cross (more a miniature indoor market than a cross) had fallen foul of the parliamentarians in 1643, but a new market house had been built by the 1650s (using money that by rights should have gone to Cromwell's army in Ireland). The importance of the building is reflected in the amount of money lavished upon it, most of which came courtesy of the Conduit Lands Trust, and it was rebuilt no fewer than three times in the 18th century. The building standing at the beginning of the century was of two storeys, an arcaded covered market below (for wet weather shopping) and rooms above. By the 1730s this had been replaced by a single-storey structure, which in turn came down in the 1790s. The third reincarnation involved the demolition of the Roundabout House, a common feature of market squares and always an inconvenience. The one in Lichfield, however, had proved itself temporarily useful for housing the city's fire engine. Once the Roundabout House had gone it was possible to rebuild the market hall on a larger scale, and the new version was complete in 1797. Even this was of limited duration; in 1849 it was pulled down yet again and replaced by a combined corn exchange and market hall in Conduit Street.

Nevertheless, Samuel Johnson's succinct summary of the ethos of his home town was substantially right. It was, or had become, a city of philosophers – and writers and thinkers and gardeners and singers – and as the 18th century ended Lichfield was about to embark upon the most glorious and influential period of its history.

CHAPTER SEVEN

Close Families

On 13 July 1771 Anna Seward wrote rapturously to a friend:

> Our rambles up on the Terrace have been very animated these last eve-
> nings. Mr Edgeworth enlivening us by a wit, exclusive as the light of
> the Sun and active as its heat, Dr Darwin laughing with us, while we
> have felt the fine edge of elegant, ingenuous and what is most rare, good
> humour'd irony … Il Penseroso Saville sighing and singing to us, sharing
> and imparting our enthusiasms … Mr Day improving our minds while
> he delights our imaginations.

Nothing conveys better the sense of eternal summer that this Georgian
society was enjoying, along with a feeling of being in the right place at the
right time. After a century in the wilderness, when aspiring writers and
thinkers deserted Lichfield for the capital, the world (and occasionally his
wife) were now heading in the opposite direction. Nor was it simply for the
assembly rooms, the waters and the tea ceremonies. Lichfield was drawing
in some of the foremost thinkers and scientists of the age. The city had
become, as Miss Seward proudly expressed it, 'a little Athens'.

The chattering classes had long been resident in Lichfield close, but now
they wrote as much as they chattered, and from the voluminous correspondence
of Richard Edgeworth, Anna Seward and Erasmus Darwin we can do more
than simply peer through the windows of this gilded world; we can join
them on the terrace and in the drawing-room.

The presiding spirits of this world were 'the Swan of Lichfield', Anna
Seward herself, and Erasmus Darwin, who lived at opposite angles of the
close. As individuals they were chalk and cheese; one a writer and social
observer, the other a physician, scientist and intellectual, but they got on
famously, sharing a love of poetry and people and gardens. 'He looks like
a butcher', said Anna of her friend, 'and I like a fat cook maid'. Neither
was a native of Lichfield, but Darwin spent nearly 25 years in the close,

49 *An engraving from the portrait of Anna Seward by Tilly Kettle (1762). In her will Anna asked to be buried 'at the feet of my late dear father, but if they should object to disturbing the choir pavement, to be laid by the side of him who was my faithful excellent friend, through the course of 37 years, the late Mr John Saville …'. She did, however, leave £500 towards a monument to her father and his family.*

while Anna Seward was there for almost 60 years, all of them spent in the same house.

Anna's father, the Rev. Thomas Seward, had been appointed in 1750 to one of the canonries of the cathedral and his family migrated from the old plague village of Eyam in Derbyshire to take up residence in the bishop's palace. The Lichfield bishops were still unwilling to live in the palace that had cost so much money, and so much ill feeling, in the previous century. Clearly the bishops were the losers in this, for Miss Seward's pen portaits of the palace and its prospects were never less than idyllic. She describes the scene to the Ladies of Llangollen thus:

> This apartment looks upon a small lawn, gently sloping upwards … It is bordered on the right hand by tall laburnums, lilacs and trees of the Gelder rose. Beyond this little lawny elevation, the wall which divides its terrace from the sweet valley it overlooks, is not visible … The vale is scarcely half a mile across, bounded, basin-like, by a semi-circle of gentle hills, luxuriantly foliaged. There is a lake in its bosom, and a venerable old church, with its grey and moss-grown tower on the water's edge. Left of that church, on the rising ground beyond, stands an elegant villa, half shrouded in its groves; – and to the right below, on the bank of the lake, another villa with its gardens.

No doubt the ladies of Plas Newydd would not have enjoyed references to the tanneries, the parchment factory and the tenters, which would also have been visible. Appreciation of the picturesque was a state of mind, and there is no more significant description of this vista than when Anna calls it 'Claude-Lorrain-like', a French landscape made real. That said, the view across to Stowe is one we can still share with Anna Seward, and it still retains much of its (largely artificial) beauty. Of the view in the opposite direction Anna is not quite as forthcoming, though it was attractive enough in a man-made sort of way. Even on his whirlwind tour of Britain Daniel Defoe had time to recognise its chief qualities:

> There are in the Close, besides the Houses of the Clergy Residentiaries, a great number of well-built and well-inhabited Houses; which makes Lichfield a Place of good Company, above all the Towns in this or the neighbouring Counties of Warwickshire or Derbyshire.

This then was the stage on which an extraordinary collection of characters were set to play their parts.

Lichfield close had not, of course, been devoid of artistic aspiration before the Sewards' time, and Anna was not slow to extol the achievements of her grandfather, the single-minded master of the grammar school, John Hunter, as well as a previous resident of her house, Gilbert Walmesley, who had been a 'Maecenas' to Johnson and Garrick:

> Two or three evenings every week Mr Walmesley called the stupendous stripling and his livelier companion, David Garrick ... to his plentiful board. There, in the hours of convivial gaiety, did he delight to waive every restraint of superiority formed by rank, affluence, polished manners and the dignity of advanced life ...

A generation later, the palace retained its reputation for learning. In his memoirs Richard Edgeworth reflected that the palace 'was the resort of every person in that neighbourhood who had any taste for letters'. Thomas Seward himself had literary ambitions, edited the plays of Beaumont and Fletcher and wrote much verse, among which a poem on woman's right to intellectual equality with man could be considered ahead of its time. He was also a great enthusiast for Shakespeare, an interest that united him with the 'stupendous stripling and his livelier companion' whom Walmesley had entertained. It was ironic that Lichfield should have nurtured both the bard's editor and his greatest interpreter, for across Stowe Pool dwelt the man who had tried his level best to erase him from the national record. In the 1750s the Rev. Francis Gastrell had been the owner of New Place, the house in Stratford-upon-Avon where Shakespeare died, though he spent much of his time in Lichfield and his curacy was actually in Cheshire. In the space of three years Gastrell first chopped down the bard's legendary mulberry tree and then demolished New Place itself, before making his move to Lichfield permanent, whither the opprobrium of the literary world (and the tour operators of Stratford) followed him. (We should add in the Rev. Gastrell's defence that little of the Tudor fabric of the house was left by his time, and that he did have to put up with sightseers climbing into his garden.) Francis and Jane Gastrell lived at Stowe House – one of the two villas Anna Seward could see from her window – where they were connected to the close society by marriage: Jane's sister had married Gilbert Walmesley. Here Boswell took tea with Mrs Gastrell in 1776, while Johnson was similarly occupied with Mrs Gastrell's sister, Elizabeth Aston, next door at Stowe Hill.

The life of the Sewards, and families like them, might by some be accounted dull, and the following letter from Anna to an unidentified friend called Emma (dated February 1763) does little to dispel that impression:

> I do not attempt to send you news; since neither love nor marriage, novel propery, or recent misfortune, have produced any change … in the situation and sentiments of those who interest you in our little city, it is time to bid you adieu. My sister has brought my workbag with her own down for the evening. My father and mother are gone to a card-party. The curtains are dropt, and the chill white world shut out. The candles shine cheerily, and the fire burns bright in the clean hearth. Little Honora draws her chair to the table as I write, Hawksworth's *Almoran and Hamlet* in her hand … Honora looks at me, her eyes sparkling with intellectual avidity.

Whether one finds such domestic bliss touching or cloying is a matter of personal taste, but it was not going to last much beyond this anyhow, for the first of a succession of dark strangers was about to enter the scene and upset the equilibrium of the close.

The Honora in question was Honora Sneyd, the daughter of a relation of the Sewards, to whom the description of the three spires as 'Ladies of the Valley' is attributed and whose upbringing had been entrusted by her widowed father to the society of the close. Anna doted on her, and grieved inconsolably for her early passing. The younger sister with the workbags was Sarah (called Sally), ear-marked for marriage with Joseph Porter, Dr Johnson's son-in-law, who was shortly to arrive from Italy to claim his prize. Such a marriage, if not exactly made in heaven, was certainly made on Parnassus, for it would have linked Anna to Samuel by genealogy, as they were certainly united by friendship. But such a marriage was not to be. Sally Seward contracted typhoid shortly before the wedding and not even the great Dr Darwin could save her.

As for Honora, there was an equally ill-fated relationship on the horizon for her. It must be remembered that Lichfield was as much a military town as it was an ecclesiastical one, and matches between sons of the army and daughters of the close were nothing out of the ordinary. The prospective groom in question was John André and, though he was not in uniform when he first met Honora, he was shortly to be so. They met in 1769. The appropriate modest glances were cast in both directions and the suitor correctly corresponded via Anna, but Honora's father disallowed the liaison, and John André married the army instead. There was one last (and sorrowful) visit to the Sewards before he retired from the scene. The subsequent news that Major André had been captured in the American War of Independence and hanged as a spy must have sent a frisson of excitement through the close.

50   *Honora Sneyd, after a drawing by George Romney. Anna wrote of the picture: 'that sweet, that sacred decency, that reserved dignity of virgin grace, which characterised her look and air, when her thoughts were tranquil, live in this dear portrait ... .' Anna could never forgive Edgeworth for taking her 'Serena' away from Lichfield, or Honora for going.*

The appearance of Richard Lovell Edgeworth (1744-1817) in Lichfield in 1766 elicited equal excitement. Edgeworth brought with him decidedly more intellectual baggage than the earlier strangers in the close, but that brilliance came at a price. He studied at both Trinity College, Dublin, and at Oxford, but had left without a degree from either, dissolute behaviour scuppering his chances at the former, the birth of a child preventing graduation at the latter. By the age of 20 Edgeworth was married (to which he was eminently unsuited), a father (likewise) and embarking on a career in practical (and impractical) mechanics. This was, after all, an age of invention and almost any man with academic pretensions tried his hand. Edgeworth's particular interest was in new modes of transport and he dabbled in velocipedes (a kind of primitive bicycle), before turning his attention to carriages. One with sails came first,

51 *Richard Lovell Edgeworth (1744-1817). Edgeworth's most significant achievement was probably his three-volume work* Practical Education, *the best guide of its time to the teaching of children. The book was a family effort: his daughter, Maria, wrote most of it, while his son and wife contributed individual chapters. It ran to three editions and was translated into Dutch.*

and after this 'a very handsome phaeton capable of being turned in a small compass'. It was suggested to Edgeworth that he make contact with Dr Darwin, who had also designed a carriage which could turn on the 18th-century equivalent of a sixpence, and so, after an initial exchange of letters, Edgeworth arrived at Darwin's house in the summer of 1765.

That first meeting was unusual enough to enter the correspondence of both Edgeworth himself and Miss Seward. Darwin was on his rounds when Edgeworth arrived and it was several hours later, spent in the company of Mrs Darwin, before the young man got to see the great man:

> When supper was finished, a loud rapping at the door announced the Doctor. There was a bustle in the hall, which made Mrs Darwin get up and go to the door. Upon her exclaiming, that they have bought in a dead man, I went into the hall. I saw some persons, directed by one whom I guessed to be Dr Darwin, carrying a man who appeared motionless. 'He is not dead,' said Dr Darwin. 'He is only dead drunk. I found him nearly suffocated in a pitch. I had him lifted into my carriage, and brought hither, that we might take care of him tonight.' Candles came, and what was the surprise of the Doctor, and of Mrs Darwin, to find that the person whom he had saved was Mrs Darwin's brother!

To make the acquaintance of Erasmus Darwin was to gain an introduction to two worlds: to the close and its women and to the scientific family, of which Darwin was a member, known as the Lunar Society. Richard Edgeworth was launched, like a carriage in full sail, into both.

To Anna Seward he was 'gracefully spirited and his conversation eloquent'; to Dr Darwin he was a magician. Twenty miles away in Handsworth, Matthew Boulton could feel Darwin's excitement:

… Edgeworth has the principles of nature in his palm and moulds them as he pleases – can take away polarity, or give it to the needle by rubbing it thrice on the palm of his hand! And can see through two solid boards without glasses! Wonderful! Astonishing! Diabolical! Pray tell Dr Small he must come to see these miracles.

Boulton and Small did indeed come forthwith to Lichfield, if more to consult Dr Darwin about pumping engines than to see a magic show. Still, Richard Edgeworth was hereby fully installed in the foremost scientific society of its day, and remained so for the rest of his life. Lichfield must have seemed to him the perfect resting-place: charm and beauty on one side and science and innovation on the other. Had he not been married and living in Berkshire, he might have settled down there and then.

While Edgeworth was considering his position, another stranger entered the Lichfield stage, perhaps the most curious of the whole bunch. This was Thomas Day (1748-89), a friend (as it happened) of Richard Edgeworth's, and like him an Oxford man. He too had been drawn to Lichfield by Darwin, but by a decidedly roundabout route. Day is a reminder that the romantic hero was being forged some time before the romantic era. His appearance, as described by Anna, appears like a re-working of her old friend, Samuel Johnson, but with more hair:

Mr Day looked the philosopher. Powder and fine clothes were, at the time, the appendages of gentlemen. Mr Day wore not either. He was tall and stooped in the shoulders, full made but not corpulent; and in his meditative and melancholy air a degree of awkwardness and dignity were blended. We found his features interesting and agreeable amidst the traces of a severe smallpox.

The chief influence upon Day's philosophy was the French writer, Jean Jacques Rousseau, whose particular take on life can be summed in his famous maxim: 'Man is born free but is everywhere in chains'. It was the opinion of Rousseau and of Day that man's (and woman's) innate innocence and beauty were corrupted by society, particularly the society on offer in the 18th century. Thomas Day applied this theory directly to his own search for a spouse. Being naturally suspicious of the kind of women Georgian England was producing, he decided to create his own, some 50 years before Mary Shelley came up with the same idea. Unable or unwilling to resort to body parts and a lightning conductor, Day chose to select a young girl, as yet unmarred by social corruption, and educate her himself, thereby fashioning the perfect

52 *Stowe House, from 1770 temporary home of Thomas Day, and a year later of the Edgeworths too. At arm's length from the city, Day found it a 'pleasant mansion' and a conveniently distant place to raise Sabrina 'in the virtues of Arria, Portia and Cornelia'. But female perfection, as Day found, was not to be attained here or in any other place.*

'designer wife'. And so in 1769 Day visited a foundling home in Shrewsbury and chose a girl (whom he christened Sabrina Sidney, after the river and his favourite author) to create that perfect match. And in case of error he chose a second girl, this time from a similar hospital in London, and called her Lucretia.

Being naturally distrustful of collateral contamination from English society, he took them to France, where the two young girls quarrelled, cried, caught smallpox and generally caused their mentor much trouble. After eight months this disfunctional family returned to England, by which time Day had already made his choice. He placed Lucretia in the care of a London milliner, with an apprenticeship indenture worth £100, allowing him to concentrate more single-mindedly on Sabrina.

Where better to perfect this piece of social engineering than in Lichfield, far from the corruption of the modern world, where truth and beauty were still unstained? In 1771 Thomas Day decided to rent Stowe House, at arm's length from the close, but close enough for association with Darwin and the

Lunar Society to which Erasmus would shortly be introducing him. Day was no scientist or inventor, but he was a thinker and the Lunar Society was wide in his field of interests. Shortly afterwards, the Edgeworths moved in as well.

Sabrina was now a teenager of 13 years, by all accounts attractive, accomplished and intelligent. But, for all his efforts and expenses, she was not to Day's taste. She was afraid of horses, keen on clothes and not at all fearless when Day brandished guns near here. Sabrina would have to go. Having despatched her to a boarding-school in Sutton Coldfield, Thomas Day began to look elsewhere for nuptial prospects.

This whole episode might seem distasteful to modern eyes, but we should recognise that exactly the same social engineering was going on in all the close families. Bringing up daughters to be refined, agreeable (but above all) eligible was what one did. Admittedly it had not worked with Anna Seward, but it had worked perfectly with Honora Sneyd, and 'matchless Honora' now became the focus not only of Thomas Day's attention, but also that of Richard Edgeworth, in spite of his marital status.

By this time Honora's father had come to live in Lichfield close, where he could assemble all his five daughters under one roof and deal more conveniently with all their respective suitors. Thomas Day came for the hand, first of Honora and then of her sister, Elizabeth. Richard Edgeworth wooed Honora. The situation was scandalous, but the close was well used to scandal. Anna Seward had been carrying on an affair with one of the vicars choral for some time. John Saville too was married, though separated from his wife. It was not – it has to be said – much of a separation, since the two continued to live next door to each other.

Like a good Jane Austen novel, it is necessary to tie up the frayed ends of these relationships. Thomas Day did not find happiness in the close. On the advice of Dr Small he moved away from Lichfield, settled in France and found a poor girl to love and marry there. But Day's delayed marital bliss was not to last long, for he died after a fall from his horse at the age of 41. He left behind him a sorrowful wife and an outstanding collection of children's stories called *Sandford and Merton*. For Richard Lovell Edgeworth there was a longer life and no fewer than four wives. The first Mrs Edgeworth died in childbirth, allowing him to marry Honora in the lady chapel of Lichfield Cathedral.

This too was a brief marriage; Honora died of consumption in April 1780, and Edgeworth returned to Lichfield to seek the hand of her sister,

53 *The cathedral from the north-west. The leafy lane between the cathedral and the houses on the north side of the close was a popular place for promenading. John André wrote to Anna Seward in 1769: 'I sympathize in your resentment against the canonical dons, who stumpify the heads of the good green people, beneath whose friendly shade so many of your happiest hours have glided away … .'*

Elizabeth. But if the close had grudgingly accepted the first betrothal, it drew the line at the second. On the advice of Matthew Boulton (who had himself married two sisters from Lichfield) Edgeworth took Elizabeth off to London to be married. Boulton reassured him:

> It will not be even one day's wonder in the Capital, nor seven days' wonder in a country town, nor more than nine days' wonder in a Cathedral card-playing town.

Thus Richard Edgeworth fades from the Staffordshire scene. His later life was spent on his Irish estate, inventing – the list includes a turnip-cutter, an umbrella for covering haystacks and an early version of semaphore – writing books on education and looking after his 22 children. Maria, his daughter by the first marriage, herself became a celebrated novelist, though she was too young to remember much of the Lichfield days (or indeed the Days of Lichfield).

Anna Seward lived on to mourn the deaths (and compose the epitaphs) of most of her contemporaries: Honora and Elizabeth Sneyd, John André, Thomas Day and John Saville. After the death of her father in 1790 she lived on in the palace, much of the time alone. Not that Anna was short of company; as the poet, William Hayley, noted while staying at the palace: 'she has a multitude of female visitors, and a host of divines'. Sadly, Miss Seward's reputation as a poet has not outlived her, but then the 18th century was not a particularly good one for poetry. In her lifetime, however, 'the Swan of Lichfield' was well respected and well published, especially after her triumphant 'Elegy on Captain Cook' in 1780. It was left to Sir Walter Scott to deal with her literary legacy and to compose the lines which commemorate her in the cathedral. They end, somewhat limply, thus:

> Lo! One brief line an answer sad supplies –
> Honour'd, belov'd, and mourn'd here Seward lies:
> Her worth, her warmth of heart, our sorrows say:
> Go seek her genius in her living lay.

For the author of 'The Lay of the Last Minstrel', the final word perhaps had more impact than it does for us.

As for Erasmus Darwin (1731-1802), he passed from Lichfield life (though not his own) in 1780, when he moved his practice to Derby. Of all the inhabitants of the close, posterity has been kindest to Erasmus and rightly so. Although his achievements have been rather overshadowed by those of his grandson, Charles, no history of Lichfield is complete without some account of the man whose contribution to science (in its widest sense) and to Lichfield, where he spent the most creative 25 years of his life, was immense. Darwin was also, as it happens, one of the most interesting characters of the 18th century and a most wonderful letter-writer.

We first met Darwin as an amateur carriage-maker, at the time when Edgeworth came to see him. By then (1765) Darwin had been living in Lichfield for nine years. He had married one of the daughters of the close (Mary Howard), and in 1760 built a new house on the west side of the close, facing Beacon Street. Moving in was Darwin's early introduction to gardening, which was to become one of his hobbies, for dividing the front of the house from the road was the medieval moat that had once encircled the close. According to Mary, her husband cleared the ditch of briars, planted lilac and roses and 'flung a broad bridge of shallow steps with Chinese paling, descending from his hall door to the pavement'.

54 *Portrait of Erasmus Darwin by Joseph Wright of Derby. Erasmus and Anna had much in common, including their love of cats. In 1780 Darwin's cat, Grimalkin, purportedly penned an epistle of love to Miss Pussy across the close, lamenting how 'the treacherous Porcupine, Cupid' had pierced his fluttering heart. Miss Pussy replied that she could never countenance a relationship with such a fierce creature.*

Carriage-making remained a hobby for many a long year, if for no better reason than Dr Darwin spent many a long year in a carriage. As a physician with a high reputation, visiting patients took up much of his time, and it has been estimated that he travelled an average of 30 miles a day, or 10,000 miles a year. It at least gave him plenty of time to think, to read and to road-test various vehicles. One that he was not able to try out was his design for a steam-driven carriage, for he could not persuade Matthew Boulton to build it. Darwin's carriages must have been a familiar sight on the roads around Lichfield, easily recognised by the family coat of arms – three scallop shells – and the legend 'E conchis omnia' (everything from sea-shells). The words were an early indication that Darwin's mind was already occupied by the subject of evolution. Such theories were not designed to go down well on the ecclesiastical side of the close. Dr Seward wrote that his neighbour

... renounces his Creator,
And forms all sense from senseless matter.
Great wizard he! by magic spells
Can all things raise from cockle shells.

There's no doubt that Darwin's skills as a physician were a huge asset to the city, not only for the rich, but also the poorer inhabitants, many of whom he attended free of charge. Darwin certainly did not need every last penny from his practice: his annual income rose from less than £200 in the 1750s to over £800 by the 1770s. Among his patients were John Saville, on whom Darwin practised successful electrotherapy, and James Brindley, the famous canal surveyor. Josiah Wedgwood comments that, of all the physicians who tended Brindley, Darwin was the first to diagnose diabetes. The presence of Dr Darwin also added to Lichfield's educational opportunities, as the following advertisement, preserved by Charles Darwin, testifies:

> October 23rd 1762. The body of the Malefactor, who is order'd to be executed in Lichfield on Monday the 25th instant, will be afterwards conveyed to the House of Dr Darwin, who will begin a Course of Anatomical Lectures, at Four o'clock on Tuesday evening, and continue them every Day as long as the Body can be preserved, and shall be glad to be favoured with the Company of any who profess Medicine or Surgery, to whom the Love of Science may induce.

Darwin was, after all, a graduate of Edinburgh, where a certain Burke and Hare also practised.

But it was always his extra-curricular activities that gave Erasmus Darwin most pleasure. As he described his life to an old student friend in Hamburg in 1768:

> I have a good House, a pleasant Situation, a sensible Wife, and three healthful Children, and as much medical Business as I can do with Ease, and rather more. Mechanics and Chemistry are my Hobby-horses ...

Darwin might have added botany, poetry, physics, geology, zoology and anthropology to the list.

Of botany we have the evidence of the water garden he planted at Abnalls, on the site of Sir John Floyer's baths, as well as the Botanic Society he founded in Lichfield. Admittedly it had only three members, but their work in translating Linnaeus was an early contribution to the classification of plants in England. Such interests reached their zenith in his didactic poems, *The Loves of Plants* (1789), *The Economy of Vegetation* (1792) and *The Botanic Garden* (1792), admired and imitated by Walpole, Coleridge and Wordsworth. It has to be said that the author's footnotes far exceed the lines of verse, but in them Darwin distilled a lifetime's scientific study and speculation, ruminating on the Earth's creation and the Descent of Man. By the time of his huge treatise, *Zoonomia*, published in 1794, it seems evident that Darwin had moved tantalisingly close to the theory of natural selection that his grandson would formulate on board the *Beagle*:

55   *Darwin House on Beacon Street. Erasmus Darwin moved here in 1758, converting a timber-framed house into something much more fashionable. Here Dr Darwin could turn his architectural (and metaphorical) back on the church, and yet keep in close touch with its staff. The stone steps replaced an earlier bridge, which allowed access to the house across the city ditch.*

> The final cause of this contest amongst the males seems to be, that the strongest and most active animal should propagate the species, which should thence be improved.

From Erasmus to Charles it was, it seems, only a matter of evolution.

Darwin's restless and inventive mind – Coleridge said of him 'that he had a greater range of knowledge than any other man in Europe' – though it courted controversy in the close, made him an indispensable member of the scientific establishment and of the Lunar Society, and the house in Beacon Street (now a museum) witnessed a procession of famous and influential visitors: James Watt, Benjamin Franklin, Richard Edgeworth, Josiah Wedgwood and James Keir all stayed there. All was done in an atmosphere of scientific enquiry, and the free exchange of ideas. Darwin demonstrated his carriages, his speaking-machine and the speaking-tube he used for communication in the house; Franklin made for him a bladder and funnel, with which Darwin could collect pond gas whilst out swimming. They spoke about balloons and canals and steam-engines and electricity. These were indeed remarkable days in Lichfield close.

The city in which the Sewards, the Darwins and their like played their part itself underwent something of a cultural renaissance in this period. Matthew Boulton might have thought it 'a card-playing town', but there were far more impressive ways to squander money. The annual Lichfield Races, transferred from Fradley Heath to Whittington Heath in 1702, was undoubtedly the social event of the year, the three days of racing accompanied by public breakfasts, assemblies, balls and dinners, the *Swan* being the most popular venue for the latter. On the course itself there were cock-fights, private horse races and running matches to supplement the main event. The Lichfield Races was not the only race meeting held in Staffordshire, but it was certainly the biggest, and a grandstand was erected on the course (by the landlord of the *Red Lion*) in 1773, probably at the height of its popularity. Soon after this a decline seems to have set in, such that by 1836 General William Dyott noted in his diary of that year:

> Lichfield March races: a complete failure, a parcel of hacks, and a hurdle race, a new fashioned sport much in vogue with the fox-hunters; a wretched affair over old Whittington.

Yet the event hung on until 1895, when the building of the Whittington Barracks made their continuation undesirable, if not actually impossible.

Luckily the race meeting was not the only event in the social calendar. Although subscription balls proliferated in race week, they were in evidence throughout the year. The guildhall was a favourite venue, as was the *George* and St James's Hall on Bore Street. When the vicars choral rebuilt their hall in the close in 1757 it re-opened with a splendid concert of music and dancing. The confined area, however – the hall was on the first floor – meant that ladies were requested not to wear hooped skirts, for fear of taking up all the available space!

The presence of the cathedral served to preserve Lichfield's long musical tradition, but the 18th century can hardly be said to have been a golden age. John Alcock, who was appointed as cathedral organist and master of the choir school in 1750, was so exasperated by the casual attitude of his colleagues in the vicars' hall that he wrote indignantly to the dean:

> ... no Choir in the Kingdom is so much neglected by its Members thereof as this; one of them attending no more than five Weeks in a Year, another five Months, some seven, and few of them so often as they might do; sometimes only one Priest-Vicar at Church, and at other times, but one Lay-Vicar, both on Sundays as well as the Week-days, tho' there are Eleven of them, which has occasion'd some People of the Town to write upon the Church Doors, My House shall be called the House of Prayer, but ye have made it a Den of Thieves ...

We might suspect that Alcock penned the graffiti himself, for Alcock's relationship with the vicars and indeed the whole cathedral hierarchy was rocky, to say the least. Alcock's attempts to reform and invigorate the cathedral's music had fallen on deaf ears and, as often happened in the close, the trouble-maker found himself ostracised. Alcock found comfort in fiction, writing a thinly veiled parody of close life, entitled *The Life of Miss Fanny Brown*, which was published in Birmingham in 1760. Alcock at least had the decency to write under a pseudonym, but his behaviour during church services hardly disguised his contempt. Consequently, the dean found himself in receipt of another petition, this time from the vicars choral themselves, requesting that their recalcitrant organist:

> ... may not show his Contempt or Indignation by playing the Chants, Services or Anthems so fast that the Choir cannot sometimes articulate half the words; or else so slow that their Breath will not serve to hold out the long, loitering, dragging Notes. That he may not hereafter mock, and mimick with his Voice any of the Vicars, as he frequently has done, in the Responses and even in the Confession. That he may not show his Splenetic Tricks upon the Organ to expose or confound the Performers, or burlesque their manner of Singing. That he may not play Full where he ought not; or so loud (in the Verses especially) that the softer Voices cannot be heard at all ...

Services in John Alcock's time must have been entertaining, if not exactly solemn.

One of the lay vicars at the time of Alcock's outcry was John Saville (d. 1803), who might have seemed the perfect embodiment of the dubious morality prevalent in the close. Saville's accomplishments as a musician were not in doubt. He took charge of music during race week, championed the cause of

Handel in the close and charmed concert-goers both as soloist and conductor across the Midlands. He certainly charmed Anna Seward (who called him 'her Giovanni'), and the two were 'close friends' for well over 30 years. As we have already said, Saville left his wife and daughters, but left them only to take up residence in a 'bachelor house' elsewhere in the close. Undoubtedly Anna and John had much in common – a mutual love of poetry, music and gardens – but scandal and disapproval hung over the relationship, especially as the dean again refused to intervene. Saville, a melancholic man by nature, therefore found solace in the spade, creating a beautiful miniature garden beside his house in the vicars' close, and then a much larger one by Stowe Pool. The latter, along with Erasmus Darwin's at Abnalls and the garden of Sir Brooke Boothby (a fellow member of the Lichfield Botanical Society) at Ashbourne Hall, were considered to be the finest in the area.

56 *Portrait of Thomas Day by Joseph Wright of Derby. James Keir said of Day that he had 'animal spirits' and 'a relish for frolic'. Neither is evident in Wright's portrait, which cost Day 40 guineas. After Day's death the painting hung in Richard Edgeworth's dining-room in Ireland. Erasmus Darwin was the painter's physician, and also sat (or stood) for him.*

Despite the fame attached to Johnson, Garrick and Farquhar, Lichfield had to wait until the end of the century for a theatre. Professional companies had been visiting the city since the 1760s, but relied on the hasty (and temporary) erection of stage and scenery at the guildhall. It needed considerable lobbying and subscriptions to effect a more permanent arrangement. The new building, designed by James Miller, opened in Bore Street in July 1790. Lichfield's literary pedigree was there for all to see on that opening night, when the curtain rose to reveal medallions of Johnson, Garrick and Anna Seward, as well as a statue of that other local playwright, William Shakespeare.

> Our Talismans are Nature, Wisdom, Grace,
> Our Genius is the Genius of this place ...

went the prologue. The genius, as it turned out, was not a desperately benevolent one. Although such thespian luminaries as Edmund Kean, Sarah Siddons and the Young Roscius trod the boards of Bore Street, not many touring companies did find their way there, and when they did it was seldom for more than a week. In between such runs local amateur companies made use of it. Theatres in far bigger places than Lichfield continually struggled to match income and expenditure, and therefore it was hardly surprising that the Theatre Royal (as it was re-named in 1859) closed in 1871. Demolition robbed the city of one of its more interesting Georgian buildings, and David Garrick would no doubt have turned in his grave, had he owned a local grave to turn in.

Such was the nature of life in and around the cathedral close. Status, leisure and learning had helped to create a world in which science, the arts and illicit affairs could be pursued with enthusiasm and the expectation of success. But it serves also to show that Lichfield had become two towns, almost as much as it had been during the Civil War, and life in the lower one was far from the bed of roses that the close had become.

CHAPTER EIGHT

A Tale of Two Cities

It is clear from the letters of Anna Seward that her affection for Lichfield stopped abruptly at the gates to the close. She found little to attract her below the pools, and even the colour and curiosities of the Greenhill Bower she thought 'grotesque and vulgar'. Town and gown were as far apart as they had ever been. But not everyone in Lichfield could afford to buy into the comfortable lifestyle on offer in the close. As in any town, poverty and deprivation stalked the many and pulled down the weakest. During the Middle Ages the cathedral would have helped to shoulder this burden, and fish, grain and eggs were being distributed to the poor by the porter in 1312. The death of a bishop or vicar might have been a personal tragedy, but often resulted in a welcome distribution of alms. On the burial of Bishop Langton in 1360, for example, no less than 1,600 of the city's poor benefited to the tune of one penny each. The Reformation had not stopped poor relief in the close, but it had certainly slowed it down. By the end of the 18th century the close was concentrating its beneficence on ex-employees, and the bread money was being given to the choristers.

Providing a safety net for those who fell out of employment down in the city was parish business and the three parishes of St Mary, St Michael and St Chad each dealt with the issue as they saw fit. Each parish had its own workhouse, but equally supported the 'outdoor' poor in their own homes. There were proposals from the 1770s for the parishes to unite their efforts and to purchase 'one commodious house' for the reception of the poor, but such a state did not finally arise until the forcible combination of the parishes under the Poor Law Amendment Act of 1834. There was some logic to the suggestion, for the three parishes differed widely in population, resources and need. By 1803 the poor rates in St Mary's parish amounted to £1,241, whilst those in St Chad's and St Michael's were £442 and £361 respectively. Such figures also reflect the numbers in receipt of poor relief: in St Mary's

57 *Lichfield union workhouse on Trent Valley Road in 1843, shortly after construction. Wards for the casual poor were added in 1874 and an infirmary in 1893. The building today still remains part of the health authority.*

184 adults and children were receiving regular support from the overseers, compared with only 37 in St Chad's and 38 in St Michael's. Demand too was irregular; the dominance of seasonal agricultural work around Lichfield each year led to a steep rise in those seeking relief once the harvest was safely gathered in.

St Mary's parish workhouse stood at the west end of Sandford Street. In the 1690s the building had been literally this, a linen manufactory where the poor of the parish were set to work, but by 1701 it was providing accommodation for paupers as well. The workhouse was managed by a married couple, and included both children, who were taught four hours a day by the master, and adults, who earned their keep by spinning cloth for local manufacturers. It also contained a 'house of correction' for offenders. By 1795, however, when Sir Francis Morton Eden was compiling his survey on *The State of the Poor*, the 41 inmates were making only 'a little blanketing for the use of the house'. He reported a monotonous diet of milk pottage for breakfast, meat and vegetables or cold meat and broth for dinner, and bread and cheese for supper, but this was during the acute economic crisis and bread shortage of the 1790s. The overseers were always under pressure to keep down the rates by selling produce from the house, and by 1803 the paupers were earning over £60 for the house, by working material supplied by a local cotton manufacturer. We may suspect that this was Sir Robert Peel, whose factory was nearby.

The poor of St Chad's and St Michael's were sharing a workhouse in the 1740s, but this arrangement was later discontinued, and St Chad's had its own building, the 'Stowe house of industry' in Stowe Street, which Eden found 'old and inconvenient'. At least such inconvenience was not experienced by many: by 1803 there were only six inmates. The workhouse for St Michael's parish was at Greenhill. The first workhouse burnt down in 1790, forcing the parish to rent part of the former *White Hart Inn* instead. This too must have been small, for it only contained four rooms on the first floor and two in the attic.

The 1834 act changed all this. Subsequent events followed a national pattern: the combining of parishes into a single poor law union, the demolition of smaller workhouses and the concentration of paupers into one institution. Initially the Lichfield Union utilised both the workhouse in Sandford Street and one at Rugeley, but plans for a new union workhouse were swiftly drawn up. (It was one of the ironies of the new system that the attempt to make poor relief more 'cost effective' usually began with massive expenditure on new buildings.) The firm of Moffat and Scott received the contract to design the new building, giving George Gilbert Scott an early introduction to the city of Lichfield, 18 years before he stamped his indelible impression upon the cathedral. (Rare is the architect who could handle these two commissions.) The site chosen was on Trent Valley Road, opposite St Michael's church, to which the inmates would soon be heading every Sunday morning. Scott's design looked like a combination of an almshouse and a medieval Oxbridge college and was thus perfectly suited to its surroundings. Opened in 1840, the building accommodated 200 inmates and cost just under £3,000 to erect. Sound investment, as it turned out, for the union workhouse formed the central core of St Michael's hospital and is still used (remarkably little altered on the outside) by the health authority today.

We should add that the poor law did not represent the only safety-net society provided. By the 1800s Lichfield boasted six friendly societies for men and two for women. Such societies provided benefits (especially to cover the cost of burial) for its members in return for regular savings, and were usually based in pubs, where some of those benefits could be squandered at the very moment of collection. In addition, as befits a cathedral town, Lichfield was awash with charities, some of which (such as that of Bishop Meuland) dated back to the Middle Ages. Typically, the bequest was the rent from property and often the gift of a Lichfield ex-resident, who had risen in status elsewhere. The majority of wills appear to restrict the dole to widows (poor men were well advised to die young), excluded those in receipt of poor relief, and more often than not comprised clothes rather than cash. Recipients of William Finney's charity, for example, wore cloaks and coats with Finney's initials prominently displayed on the sleeve. Many of these charities by the late 18th century were being administered by the corporation, which at least helped to lengthen the agenda at council meetings.

There was also, of course, the Conduit Lands Trust to help, either by distributing some of is own income, or that of charities it helped to administer. Famously in 1731, for example, the Trust was supporting Michael Johnson, 'a decayed tradesman', to the tune of ten guineas, and in the previous year the Trust was paying out:

> 15s to widow Palmer of Stowe Street, she having a large sick family
> 30s for the use and benefit of a Lame Boy, a son of Thomas Smith, a poore inhabitant
> Peter Read having broke his arm 2s 6d
> Pd ye constable for looking after ye mother of ye Dead Child that was found £3
> Two guineas for cloathing Benj. Palmer, a poore natural.

The last entry here serves to remind us that in the eyes of many lunacy was close to poverty, severely impairing a person's ability to support himself. A number of the inmates of the Lichfield workhouses would have been classed as such, although in the close confines of the Lichfield institutions they were unlikely to have received the separate care they were often given elsewhere. The Poor Law Amendment Act specified that 'dangerous lunatics' should be transferred to an asylum, but the terms of the act were ambiguous and some inmates found themselves being shuffled endlessly between workhouse and asylum. Ultimately the decision was usually based on the cost of upkeep. Until the 1840s (when a series of parliamentary acts forced the local authorities to build a county or borough asylum) a lucrative trade in private madhouses was carried on, accommodating patients from a wide area. A Lichfield physician, George Chadwick, had converted his house in St John Street into one such by 1775. (This may have begun as a purely domestic arrangement, since Mrs Chadwick was one of the inmates by the 1780s.) Such houses

58 *The entrance to the Bishop's Palace in 1953, shortly before the house was relinquished to accommodate the Cathedral School. The palace was built in 1686-7 (although no work was allowed on Sundays) and cost almost £4,000. Dean Addison described it as 'strong enough for generations, and for comeliness and convenience fit to receive a person of quality'.*

required an annual licence and were subject to regular inspection by justices, and it is from these reports and those of the Metropolitan Commission for Lunacy that we can learn something of the nature of the regime. The conditions inside Chadwick's were evidently far from perfect, for its licence had been withdrawn by 1814. Enter then Dr Thomas Rowley, who gained considerable income and an equal amount of notoriety, from his trade as a private madhouse keeper in the first half of the 19th century.

Rowley initially set up in business in a property adjoining Chadwick's in 1817, but within three years had transferred to new and more spacious surroundings at Sandfields. Like other such institutions Sandfield House catered for both private and poor law patients, and in 1850 there were 13 private and 31 pauper inmates. Interestingly, there is more evidence of dissatisfaction from corporate clients than private ones. The Warwick board of guardians found it necessary to voice their criticisms of the treatment of patients at Sandfield in 1839, reporting that:

... a man named Harrison was lying upon Straw placed upon some Bedstead in a small room without any covering and in a perfect state of nudity fastened down by one arm and one Leg to the Bedstead. That another man named Gilks was in a very dirty state having his mouth full of soil and appearing not to have been shaved for some days.

Opinions as to the desirability of 'mechanical restraint' differed widely, but the presence of a beard and unhygienic conditions were universally frowned upon. The Lichfield magistrates held an immediate enquiry over the state of Sandfield, at which Dr Rowley's behaviour was said to be 'unbecoming so serious a subject', yet his licence was not at this time withdrawn. Indeed, it was not revoked for another 17 years, despite almost annual criticism. The report of the Metropolitan Commissioners in December 1855 finally obliged the magistrates to act. They wrote:

> The rooms occupied by the Pauper and poorer Patients are small, dirty, gloomy and destitute of comfort. The yards are very small, and insufficient for the purpose of exercise. The beds and bedding are for the most part in the worst state, the beds and mattresses being thin, and many of them being full of knots. The blankets, some of which are in fragments, are thin, and quite insufficient for this cold season. Much of the bedding is soiled. Some of the floors are wet, and saturated with urine.

The report went considerably further than this, but there was already enough evidence to spell the end for one of Lichfield's less savoury institutions. It was the last of the private madhouses in the West Midlands to close, though whether this was a cause of satisfaction is another matter.

Georgian and Victorian Lichfield was, to borrow an old cliché, a place of contrasts. But unlike a growing metropolis such as nearby Birmingham, in Lichfield old and new, rich and poor dwelt cheek-by-jowl. There is no better place to see such contrasts than in the middle of Bore Street. What is now the Tudor Cafe reflects the vernacular architecture of the late 16th century, complete with first-storey jetty and herring-bone studding. Next to this Donegal House, built in 1730 for James Robinson, a wealthy Lichfield merchant, represents Georgian town housing at its best. The architect was probably Francis Smith of Warwick, who designed nearby Trentham Hall. And next to this stands the Guildhall, though not the one which stood here in the 18th century, which functioned as a prison, fire-engine house, an oil house for the storage of lamp oil, theatre, banqueting hall and meeting room for the corporation, to name only a few of its uses.

Since the dissolution of the medieval guild a succession of buildings at the junction of Bore Street and Breadmarket Street had embodied Lichfield's civic authority, established and confirmed by a sequence of royal charters. Superficially there was considerable kudos attached to this body; they processed and feasted well (especially during race week), kept on good terms

59 *The Corn Exchange, which opened in 1849. The building served a variety of purposes. The Lichfield Savings Bank occupied the Conduit Street end (to the left of this picture), whilst a market hall (specialising in butter and poultry) faced onto the market square. On the upper floor dealers bought and sold corn. Outside working hours the building has served as a skating rink, a Salvation Army meeting hall and a centre for adult education.*

with the local nobility, and remained staunchly comfortable and conservative. Any member whose finances were not in good order was likely to find himself removed from office. The membership met frequently, if irregularly, in a room on the first floor of the guildhall, where they discussed a limited range of issues, primarily what to do with the money raised from market tolls and corporate rents. In reality, however, the corporation had very limited horizons and even more limited resources. Even the extensive alterations to the guildhall, undertaken in the early 1700s and again in the 1730s, were paid for not by the tenants but by the Conduit Lands trustees. The corporation in general preferred a cheaper 'supervisory' role.

The confusing overlap of powers between the Trust and the Corporation became even more problematic with the passing of the Improvement Act of 1806. Like many other boroughs in England, Lichfield took advantage of parliamentary legislation to draw up a bill 'for paving, cleansing, watch, lighting and regulating the streets, lanes and other public passages' which required the appointment of improvement commissioners. The work of this third body was restricted to the responsibilities specified in the act (though this allowed considerable scope), and the costs borne by a rate levied in each ward, of which there were fourteen. The commissioners themselves could not employ labour directly, having to contract out everything from the lighting of lamps to the collection of rates, but over the space of 30 odd years they had a significant impact on the lives of all Lichfeldians.

60 *A procession of sheriffs leaves the cathedral after a service in December 1953. During the 18th century the cathedral clergy tended to turn their backs on the town, both ecclesiastically and socially. Such a division was made all the more obvious by the restorations of James Wyatt in the late 1780s, when the chancel was effectively screened off and separated from the nave. The opening up of the building by the Victorian architects was matched by the increased number of services.*

Immediately on entering office the commissioners said 'let there be light'. Street lighting was a duty the Conduit Lands trustees had taken upon themselves, and over the course of the 18th century the number of oil lamps provided had risen from 34 in 1767 to 134 at the end of the century, though this was supplemented by a number of lamps outside private houses. This number was to be doubled once the commissioners took over responsibility, and a London contractor called Thomas Couldery arrived to 'light, trim, snuff, cleanse, supply and maintain' the 250 new lamps to be fitted around the city. For this he received 14s. 9d. per lamp, provided that they burned until 2.00 in the morning, lighting-up time varying depending on the time of year. No lights were required during the summer months or for the week of the full moon, and the moon continued to be an excuse for saving fuel even into the era of gas-light. Perhaps the moon was especially bright in Staffordshire.

Neither the commissioners nor the municipal council that followed them were especially quick at grasping the opportunities of new technology. Proposals for lighting the city by gas were around from the 1820s, but it was not until the formation of the Lichfield Gas Company in 1835 (a speculative venture by an architect, a surgeon and a grocer) that this idea became a reality. The gas works in Sandford Street continued to supply the city with coal gas for the next 90 years. Electricity had to wait until the 1920s.

Cleansing was another part of the act which the commissioners took up with energy. It is easy to forget, seeing the elegance of Georgian buildings today, that at the time they fronted streets that were foul-smelling and polluted. Brick sewers had already been laid along Lichfield's main streets by the 1770s, but much of the drainage still involved open channels and cesspools. By 1807 a new network of culverts was being constructed by the commissioners along Bird Street and Bore Street, Conduit and Dam Street. Where the sewage was ending up (probably at a pool at the end of Quoniams Lane) was another matter, but it was at least travelling out of sight. For the waste that could not be culvetted away, the commissioners put to work a team of scavengers, though this was later reduced to a single individual. The man concerned was required to sweep the streets all day on Tuesdays and Saturdays, for which he received performance related pay. He could, however, recycle and profit by whatever he collected. Scavenging was a profession that supported thousands in the Victorian black economy.

The punishment of offenders remained an area of the corporation's jurisdiction, even in the period of improvement. Given the presence of the prison on the ground floor of the guildhall, the corporation could claim quite literally to be on top of the situation. Indeed, during the 1830s the gaoler's salary was meant to cover both management of the prison below and the guildhall above. (In 1832 he was also the city's 'special constable and police officer' and had a licence to brew beer.) The gaol itself dated back to medieval times, but reconstruction was in progress in the 1740s and more new cells were added in 1801. John Howard, who published his survey of prisons in 1774, found the conditions distasteful, but Howard was not easy to please:

> Two close cells 6.5 feet by 5.5 feet and 8 feet high. To these are added two new ones, and two rooms for debtors; a court is enclosed, in which is an offensive sewer. Act for preserving the health of prisoners not hung up. No water; no straw. Keeper's salary £2; fees 13s. 4d. No table. Allowance 1s. 6d. a week.

Additional rooms were available by the 1830s, but not necessarily in use. There were only two prisoners at the gaol in 1773, and only three in 1848. In that year government inspectors were urging its closure and the transfer of prisoners to Stafford, a move that finally took place in 1866. Some sense of what the 18th-century gaol was like can still be appreciated, since a number of the cells were opened as a museum in 1986.

The apprehending of criminals was the responsibility of the watch, and night watchmen patrolled the city, especially during race week and the winter months, when darkness made crime more likely. Watchmen were still prowling the city and suburbs in 1847, long after the formal establishment of a police force. However, law and order in Victorian Lichfield was never the contentious issue it was in towns such as Wolverhampton and Birmingham. In 1833 the city was described as 'orderly and quiet' and even in 1851 could make do with one superintendent and six constables, operating from the former *George IV* inn in Bore Street. The strength had actually been reduced by 1860, when the Inspector of Constabulary reported the local force to be 'inefficient through weakness'. Perhaps that explains the low rate of arrests. Only six indictable offences were reported in the year, along with 31 arrests for drunkenness and disorderly behaviour.

The guildhall itself was re-built in 1846, courtesy of the Conduit Lands Trust, clearing away an outdated Georgian structure and replacing it with an up-to-date medieval one, which still remains today. The tide of Gothic revival was sweeping across the city at this time: St Mary's was reconstructed with

61 *The market place in 1853, from a watercolour by W. G. Herdman. Glass was added to the arcading of the Corn Exchange in the late 1880s, and in the 1970s the ground floor was occupied by shops. The area around St Mary's church continues to function as a market place today, continuing an 850-year tradition.*

a Victorian Gothic tower and spire (in 1853) and interior (1868-70), while the cathedral underwent similarly radical alterations during the 1840s and 1850s.

It will be seen from the above that the 19th century was marked by a complicated jockeying for power between the various bodies responsible for the running of Lichfield. Twice during the 1830s and 1850s the reformed corporation failed in attempts to wrest control from the Conduit Lands Trust. But whatever it thought of the Trust's tendency to 'fritter away its

62 *Sandford Street in 1905, with the white façade of the* George Hotel *at the far end of the street. This was one of Lichfield's principal working streets, specialising in tanning, dyeing and cloth-making. Sir Robert Peel's cotton manufactory was established here in 1802, and a nearby row of 14 houses was occupied by his workers.*

income on ill-advised expenses' the corporation did not seek to challenge the Trust's time-honoured concern with the supply of water to the city and close. Another body entirely was about to do that.

The Conduit Lands had been supplying the city with water from the springs at Aldershawe for 300 years, via a conduit in Bird Street (the Crucifix), another in Market Square (Cross conduit) and a third at the corner of Tamworth Street and Lombard Street (Stone Cross). By 1806 only the Crucifix conduit remained in use, just as the city began to face up to perhaps the first water shortage in its history. The increase in population in Lichfield during the 19th century was small compared with that of surrounding towns but it was tangible enough. Overall the city grew by around 65 per cent, from 4,842 in 1801 to 7,902 in 1901, most of the increase being in the parishes of St Michael's and St Chad's. The clean water was surely responsible for the low death rate, but demand was beginning to outstrip supply, which by the 1850s was down to 18,000 gallons a day. A new reservoir was built at Greenfield in 1820, and a much larger source was tapped at Trunkfield Brook in 1853. In 1868 these were yielding around 175,000 gallons a day, but Lichfield's breweries were thirsty consumers and the supply remained inadequate. Indeed, two of the companies drilled for their own water.

But if Lichfield was experiencing unaccustomed difficulties with water, they were as nothing compared to the traumatic situation in the Black Country. Here the water supply was not only inadequate, it was also seriously polluted both by industrial contamination and by sewage. To their rescue came one John Robinson McClean, whom we will meet later as the engineer to the South Staffordshire Railway Company. In a move reminiscent of modern-day mergers between public services, McClean aimed to supply the area both with public transport and 'McClean water'. Water would be piped from the unpolluted brooks in Lichfield to Walsall, Dudley and Wednesbury, and the South Staffordshire Waterworks Co. (established in 1853) mirrored both the name and the route of the earlier railway undertaking.

It might appear perverse that, at a time of local shortage, a new company should step in to sell off what water the city had, but McClean had his eyes on a source that seems to have escaped the notice of the Trust. There were, as you may have noticed, two large pools in the centre of Lichfield, which received bounteous daily supplies from the Trunkfield and Leomansley brooks. Here, it seems, God had already provided the reservoirs that the new water company needed.

To be fair to the trustees, the reputation of Stowe and Minster Pool was not high. The former had to a large extent silted up and the latter (which needed almost constant cleaning) was the lucky recipient of diocesan sewage from the close. As awareness of public health issues grew in the 1840s there was a tendency to blame the pools for whatever sickness the city was suffering from. Dampness was something Lichfield had enjoyed for centuries, but now dampness was perceived as the close companion of disease. A local physician, James Rawson (who was responsible for the repairs to St Chad's Well), went as far as to recommend the filling-in of both pools. But McClean did not fear to tread where local interests held off. It was only, after all, a matter of money.

So it was that the two pools were leased to the South Staffordshire Waterworks Co. in 1855, and work began emptying, cleaning and re-filling them. The status of the Minster Pool in all this was somewhat uncertain; the company did not need it as a reservoir, preferring Stowe Pool for that, but they would clearly not be allowed to fill it in, whatever Dr Rawson might have wished. The scheme was completed in three years. Water was piped beneath what is now Beacon Park, under Bird Street and Minster Pool into Stowe Pool; from here it went to a pumping station at Sandfields, where it was pumped by steam power to the Black Country, which now received 250,000 gallons of fresh water per day. Once up and running, it was probably inevitable that the company would sooner or later take over the supply of water to Lichfield itself. That was the case in 1930, and in 1963 the Conduit Lands Trust sold its remaining shares in the water undertaking, thus severing a link of over 400 years.

The impact of all this upon the face of Lichfield was considerable. The two mills that had stood on Dam Street and at Stowe for perhaps a thousand years were summarily pulled down. Stowe Pool, now considerably enlarged and deepened, was given a 'promenade' along which the people of the city could enjoy a walk that had not been possible since the Middle Ages. Sewage from the close no longer drained into Minster Pool and the surroundings were turned into public gardens. As for the marshy ground – known as Swan Moggs – on the far side of Bird Street, this too was filled in and landscaped as a recreation ground.

The new park became the focus for considerable civic activity and improvement in the years that followed. While the grounds were still being laid out the corporation took advantage of the Free Libraries and Museums Act of 1857 to build a public library (with a museum and art gallery) on an adjacent site in Bird Street. Since adoption of the act was voluntary (both by council and rate-payers) it showed considerable commitment by the corporation to pursue it; Lichfield was only the second authority in the country to do so. In retrospect it may been wiser to have spent a little longer considering the library's location, for the marshy ground was a far from ideal site for any building, let alone one that contained books and manuscripts. Ultimately it had to be abandoned. The fountain, presented by Thomas James Law, the chancellor of the diocese, in 1871, was probably a more appropriate installation in the gardens, as was (given visible sinking of the library) the statue of Edward John Smith, the captain of the *Titanic*. Chancellor Law was a remarkably generous benefactor when it came to public art. Not only did he pay for the statue of Samuel Johnson in the market place (a gift of 1838) he also commissioned one of Lichfield's more unusual public monuments across the city in St Michael's churchyard. Resembling a canopied medieval tomb, the structure was surmounted by a clock with two dials which were illuminated at night by gas. As a mausoleum it was somewhat premature (Law did not die until at least 12 years after its construction), but it did serve to remind travellers on their way to Trent Valley station both of the current time and their own mortality.

Time had become a pressing concern during the 1850s. Until that point local time in England varied according to the position of the sun, and in theory Lichfield was some eight minutes behind London. The arrival of the railways had made some form of standardisation desirable, and by 1847 the rail companies were operating a single agreed timetable. But how was that time to be disseminated throughout the city? The cathedral bells marked the hours, but the tower did not have a clock, and the demolition of St Mary's tower and spire (which did) in 1853 was, quite literally, untimely. The need to address this problem coincided with the civic renaissance outlined above, and in 1856 grandiose plans were drawn up by the corporation for a clock tower. The initial plan was to erect a tall gothic canopy, with timepiece attached, over the statue of Dr Johnson in the market place. If such a memorial was good enough for Walter Scott in Edinburgh, it was good enough for Lichfield's most famous son. Given the corporation's earlier complaint about 'ill-advised expenses', it shows astonishing double

63 *The Conduit Clock in its original location at the junction of Bird Street, Bore Street and St John Street. Having provided the city with water and light, time was the last element the Conduit Lands Trust could bestow. When it was built the clock tower commemorated the 300th anniversary of the Trust.*

standards that the Conduit Lands trustees should be asked to find the money for it, but so they were. The Trust, however, had other ideas. By the time the tower was finally built in 1863 it was not over Dr Johnson, but above the Crucifix conduit in Bird Street, and the style had regressed from gothic to romanesque. Nevertheless, it was far and away the tallest building in the town centre, costing the Trust over £1,200.

The heated debate that had marked the campanile's construction did not cool with its erection. The owner of the Friary complained that the side of

64 *The tomb of Thomas James Law, chancellor of the diocese and master of St John's Hospital. Built initially for his wife (who died in 1864), it shows something of the obsession with correct time-keeping in mid-Victorian Lichfield. The monument still survives in St Michael's churchyard, close to Trent Valley Road, though the cemetery itself is rather more 'romantic' than its well-manicured appearance here.*

the tower facing west did not have a clock on it, and a fourth face was hastily added to the design, even though the Friary would be the only building to benefit from it. The argument says something about the development (or lack of it) on the west side of the city at this date. Nor was the clock especially accurate either; the man employed to wind the mechanism was obliged to make daily visits to Trent Valley station, where a railway guard brought the correct time on the London train. And even when these problems had been ironed out, the choice of location for the tower was not a happy one. From the Middle Ages through to the era of the turnpike the narrowness of St John's Street and Bird Street had always caused traffic congestion, and this became even more acute with the construction of The Friary in 1926. Splendid as it was, the clock tower only added to the chaos. It was therefore sold to the corporation and moved 500 metres or so westwards to the island at the junction with Friary Avenue, where it still stands, declaring the time to a generation raised on the wrist-watch and radio.

CHAPTER NINE

Trains and Boats and Planes

Soon shall thy arm, unconquered steam, afar,
Drag the slow barge or drive the rapid car,
Or on wide-waving wings expanded bear,
The flying chariot thro' the fields of air.

At the time they were written, Erasmus Darwin's lines might have seemed like the ramblings of a man who been out in the full moon for too long. But England first and Lichfield later were indeed about to witness a transport revolution. It might not include the steam-driven aeroplane, but all else was possible. The world of mail coaches and stage waggons was about to be overturned, as the vehicles themselves often were. The 'slow barge' was the first to arrive.

It probably would not have been wise to discuss the subject of canals too indiscriminately in Georgian Lichfield. Certainly the landlord of any of the city's coaching inns would not be too pleased to hear it. But the national mood was in advance of the Lichfield innkeepers, and 'inland navigations' came to dominate the newspapers, the landscape and the business of parliament in the second half of the 18th century. The canal was both the means to economic expansion and a considerable investment opportunity. It was the internet of the 1760s.

It is ironic that the city least subject to the allure of the canal came close to being the first place in England to have one. Lichfield might have been a coaching city and a conservative one at that, but it was not devoid of ambition and Lichfeldians knew all there was to know about the power of water. In 1758, three years before James Brindley was commissioned to cut the first canal of the modern era in Manchester, he was invited to survey a similar project in the West Midlands. Brindley examined the route of a potential navigation from the Minster Pool (an ideal canal basin if ever there was one) to the River Trent at King's Mills in Donnington. The idea behind the scheme, set out in an anonymous prospectus, was to reduce the cost of transporting goods from the manufacturing towns of Birmingham, Walsall and Wolver-hampton to the Trent and Humber. The inclusion of Lichfield was recognition of its importance at the centre of the road network and its proximity to the industrial heartlands of the West Midlands. No doubt it also indicates that Lichfield men – perhaps Erasmus Darwin and other members of the Lichfield Turnpike Trust – were backing the proposal. The leaflet concludes with the claim:

> ... that Lichfield is the Center of all the great Trading Towns above-mentioned, and therefore appears to be the properest Place to which the Navigation can be extended.

James Brindley estimated the cost of the 23-mile navigation at £16,490, including a lock between Minster and Stowe Pool and another lock at the far end of Stowe. Such a canal would certainly have transformed the city, at least in the short term, into a major transport interchange; the two pools it would have altered irrevocably. As it was it came to nothing. Lichfield was never to have a canal running through the centre of the town, even if the canal age did not entirely leave the city land-locked.

If Darwin was behind the first scheme, he soon had a much larger one to chew over. It is probable, even at the time he was surveying the canal from Minster Pool, that James Brindley and his backers had a much more extensive network in mind, the centrepiece of which was to be a canal to link the Trent and Mersey. Not one to waste his work, Brindley planned to incorporate one section of the earlier scheme – from Alrewas to King's Mills – in the new plan. The Trent & Mersey (or Grand Trunk) Canal would run from Runcorn, through Cheshire and the Potteries, to a little north of Lichfield, where it would turn north-east to join the Trent south of Derby. Inevitably the scheme attracted the wholehearted support of Josiah Wedgwood, who had constantly lamented the damage to his goods in transit by road, and he had the enthusiastic backing of Darwin too: 'I am quite charm'd with your zeal in the Public spirited scheme', Wedgwood wrote to Erasmus in June 1765.

Darwin's interest was not entirely altruistic. Together with three local manufacturers – John Barker, Robert Gage and Samuel Garbett – Darwin was planning to build an ironworks alongside the new canal at Wychnor, tapping into water power from the Trent. The expertise of the group complemented each other perfectly: Barker was a banker, a Lichfield bailiff and treasurer of the Turnpike Trust; Gage owned a paper mill at Elford and was a fellow member of the Trust; while Garbett was a powerful Birmingham industrialist, specialising in iron. Garbett's interest in the project stemmed from his dissatisfaction with the quality of bar iron then produced in England. He foresaw the possibility of importing American or Russian iron up the Humber and Trent and then by canal to Wychnor. Here the iron could be converted into rods or sheets and sold on to the manufactories of Birmingham and the Black Country. Supplying water to the mill would involve cutting a channel across the route of the Lichfield-Burton turnpike but, given Darwin's and Barker's fingers in this pie too, this was hardly going to cause a problem.

Once royal assent was received for the Trent & Mersey in 1766, a host of related schemes, including the Wychnor ironworks, became possible. It was a reflection of Lichfield's wealth that investors in the city subscribed no less than £56,000 to the canal, almost three times the sum raised in the Potteries. Whether those investors saw real local benefits or were simply climbing aboard a very lucrative bandwagon is another issue. The promoters of canals were no less inscrutable, keeping their cards close to their chest; hints at additional branches and connections were often made to attract investors and then subsequently dropped. As Wedgwood wrote in March 1767: 'We have several Navigation schemes in embryo, one from the Grand Trunk to Coventry, Banbury and I don't know where.' Such indeed was the vague promise of a branch line which was to lead from the Trent & Mersey Canal to Lichfield, Tamworth and Birmingham. A real possibility in 1767, it was dead in the water by 1770. A further scheme, launched by Garbett in 1770, to link the Black Country to the Grand Trunk via Lichfield and Fradley also came to nothing.

By the 1780s it must have appeared that the city and the people who had foreseen the potential of inland navigation earlier than most had missed the boat. With all the major canals now in place none of them had come closer to Lichfield than the Grand Trunk itself, and that was 20 miles away. Transport costs had undoubtedly been reduced – the costs of carriage from Lichfield to Manchester were down from £4 per ton (by road) to a little over £1 (by road and canal) – but carriers must have increasingly been wondering whether anyone would be bringing goods to Lichfield in the first place. Lichfield was no manufacturing centre and the places that were had found new ways and new directions to move their stock.

Later in the decade, however, there was a turn for the better. By 1788 the Coventry Canal, which had earlier run out of money, had finally reached

65 *The Wyrley & Essington Canal, with Borrowcop Hill and St Michael's church. The Lichfield stretch of the canal was closed in 1954 and parts of it were subsequently in-filled. Although it cost £90,000, the canal never truly fulfilled its promise; poor returns on tolls were supplemented by selling water to neighbouring canal companies.*

Fradley on the Grand Trunk. This was still a couple of miles east of the city, but at least it was on the Lichfield-Burton turnpike, and a wharf was established at Streethay for the transfer of goods. Finally, in 1797, came the last of the Black Country canals – the Wyrley & Essington – weaving its way through the coalfields to join the Coventry Canal at Huddlesford Junction. The route took it just to the south of the city centre. Given its cost (perhaps £90,000) and its height (there was a drop of 30 locks from Borrowcop Hill down to Huddlesford) the long-term prospects for the 'curly Wyrley' were not good. In the short term, Lichfield at last had access to the cheap coal that Birmingham had been enjoying for 30 years. By 1817 a total of 606 boats were said to be unloading over 10,000 tons of coal annually, and there were six wharves in the city waiting to receive it. The 1902 OS map shows St John's Wharf and Gallows Wharf straddling Upper St John Street, where the canal crossed the road.

That said, after almost half a century of speculation and investment, all Lichfield had to show for the canal boom was cheap coal. For the poor of the city this was not a negligible matter, but it hardly matched the vision of Erasmus Darwin and the Turnpike Trust. Worse still, the people of Lichfield do not even have the Wyrley & Essington to enjoy today. The canal was abandoned in 1954 and parts of it were subsequently filled in or built over, leaving little more than a shadow on the landscape. However, a renewed awareness of the canal as a local amenity in the late 1980s led to a remarkable attempt to reconstruct the waterway, albeit on a new line in parts. The Lichfield and Hatherton Canal Restoration Trust was established in 1992 to raise funds for the reconstruction of both the Hatherton branch of the old Staffordshire & Worcestershire Canal and the Wyrley & Essington to Huddlesford. In many ways this was as much of a crusade as attracting the canals to the city in the first place.

The phrase 'public benefit', employed so liberally by Wedgwood whilst he was promoting the Trent & Mersey Canal, was in use again in the 1840s, this time in connection with the railways. The Prime Minister and MP for Tamworth, Sir Robert Peel, voiced it as he cut the first piece of turf for the Trent Valley Railway on 13 November 1845. Public benefit may indeed have been the terminus, but the Staffordshire railways stopped en route at the stations of greed, ambition and ruthless capitalism. In his speech Peel also compared the scheme to that of the ancient Romans, almost two thousand years earlier, to drive their road from London to Chester. It was a reasonable comparison, except that the Romans worked rather more quickly and single-mindedly.

Lichfield had signalled its ambition to be a part of the railway revolution as early as 1836, with the setting up of an *ad hoc* committee under the chairmanship of the banker, Richard Greene, but local initiatives took second place to the strategies of the railway companies, who had the bigger picture in mind. The original proposition, made to the committee of the Manchester South Union Railway Company, was for a line through the town to a station and goods yard near Lombard Street. This proposal came to nothing, since parliamentary approval was not granted, and two more railway companies suffered the same frustration in the years that followed. Only with a fourth bill, shepherded through Westminster by the Prime Minister himself, did such a scheme come to fruition, by which time the Trent Valley line had radically changed its route. It now grazed the boundary of the city, with a station at Streethay, where the line crossed the Burton Road. Nor was the line any longer the property of the Trent Valley Railway Co. The directors had already sold out to the London & Birmingham Railway, and they in turn had merged with others to form the London & North Western Railway. Once these take-overs were complete Lichfield was officially and formally

66 *The railway bridge over St John Street in 1849. The line from Walsall through Lichfield to Wichnor had only recently opened, and the novelty of steam still held its attraction for passers-by! The stone for the bridge was supplied by the Earl of Lichfield. Viewed from the city side, the arms of four of the bishops – Clinton, Hacket, Hayworth and Lonsdale – were displayed above the side arches, with the city's coat of arms in the centre.*

connected to the great line running from London to Crewe. It was an exciting prospect, but passengers alighting at the new station would soon realise that Lichfield was not at the centre of the action. Cabs and omnibuses ferried them the mile or so into the city.

Luckily for Lichfield, this was far from the end of the story. Hardly a day went past in 1845 without a new railway company announcing new lines and new connections, and the city was in the sights of at least two of them. The South Staffordshire Junction Railway was planning a route between the Black Country and the Birmingham & Derby Railway at Alrewas, while the Trent Valley, Midland & Grand Junction Railway was proposing a line from Wolverhampton to Wychnor, where it would join the Midland Railway. Both companies had enlisted support from the great and the good of the city to further their cause: Richard Greene was a committee member of the latter and George Anson, one of the local MPs, was a major shareholder, while the SSJR had in its ranks various members of the Dyott family and the present mayor of Lichfield, Thomas Ready.

The technical details of the lines are less interesting than the arguments marshalled in favour of a closer connection between Lichfield and the Black Country. Those who gave evidence before the parliamentary committee in favour of the SSJR argued first that Lichfield lacked sufficient railway accommodation and that the cost of sending parcels to Walsall had doubled with the decline of the coaching trade. Secondly, it was maintained that additional trains would increase the number of visitors to the city, and thirdly that the supply of garden produce to the Black Country was being severely hampered by the lack of a convenient rail link:

> The present mode of conveyance is by carts, which occasions great expense and loss of time. The market gardeners generally leave at 12 o'clock at night and do not return until 5 or 6 the following evening. This occasions a great cost also to the consumer.

Lichfield had indeed become a regional centre for market gardening. Something like 1,300 acres of the town were under the spade by the 1840s, producing mainly potatoes, peas, onions and other root vegetables, and 70 gardeners were carting their produce to Birmingham and the Black Country.

Faced with two equal and opposite causes, Parliament split the difference, allowing one company to build the southern half of the route and the other to construct the northern part. If Westminster was subtly suggesting that the two companies might like to settle their argument with a merger, the committees took the hint and did so.

Within the space of two years, then, Lichfield found itself with three stations. Two were at Streethay, allowing that all-important connection (albeit on foot) between the South Staffordshire line and the Trent Valley, and the third lay east of St John Street. If the Euston Arch in London marked the triumphal entry to that station, then the bridge over St John Street was clearly seen as an equally powerful symbol of Lichfield's place in the new scheme of things. Designed by Thomas Johnson, a local architect, it looked like a replacement for the medieval gates to the city that Lichfield had lost over the centuries. There were two castellated towers, battlements and a veritable gallery of local heraldry. Coats of arms of bishops, landowners (and members of the railway committee) proudly welcomed the traveller to the brave new world of revived medievalism. The city station itself, just to muddy the chronological waters still further, was in Tudor style, as was the one at Trent Valley.

The first train ran on 9 April 1849, and after its successful departure 150 guests joined a celebratory banquet at the *George Inn*. Erasmus Darwin was quoted, Staffordshire was dubbed 'the California of England' and the artisans of the Black Country were invited to sample the green fields and pure air of Lichfield. They were, after all, shortly to be enjoying Lichfield water and an increased supply of Lichfield vegetables. The failure of the Manchester company to deliver the rolling stock in time for the opening of the line was not commented upon.

This might have seemed like the closing of a chapter, but (unlike today) the Victorian railways rarely stayed still for long. Within a year the company had leased the whole of the South Staffordshire line to the engineer, John Robinson McLean, who intended to use it to open up the Cannock Chase coalfields. It was the first time that a single individual had received parliamentary approval to run a railway company. McClean in turn was bought out by the LNWR in 1861, who used the line as a pawn in their battle against the Midland Railway. Finally, there was time for one last new line to find its way to Lichfield. In 1884 the Birmingham-Sutton Coldfield line was extended to Lichfield, necessitating a reconstruction of the city station and substantial alterations to the St John Street bridge. They did, however, retain the coats of arms.

As had been predicted at its opening, the line from Walsall opened up the city to excursion traffic, injecting much needed tourist money into the local economy. The Whitsun Bower was the principal attraction, but on such an occasion the train clearly struggled to take the strain:

> Cattle trucks were next tried but as the rising generation took to 'mooing' at the Passengers while the train was stationary, the dislike to using such vehicles, even at the low rate adopted, caused the plan to be withdrawn.

Little evidence of Lichfield's early railway history can be seen today. The LNWR built a new Trent Valley station in 1871, retaining the earlier one as the station-master's house until it was demolished 30 years later. The city station was substantially rebuilt in 1884 to accommodate the new line from Birmingham, and the line to Walsall was closed to passengers in 1965. By the close of the 20th century Lichfield had reverted to type, once more appearing to be an afterthought in the railway timetables, a fact made clear by Virgin Rail's removal of the early morning train to London. The Cross-City line, electrified in the late 1980s and formerly stretching from Redditch to Trent

67   *City (or South Staffordshire) Station shortly after the opening of the line in 1849. The original station was a little further along Station Road (and nearer to St Michael's church) than the current one. The building also housed the offices of the South Staffordshire Railway Company. In all, 766 navvies were engaged on the line from Walsall.*

Valley, did benefit from substantial investment in the public transport infrastructure of the area, but it was more in evidence to the south of Birmingham than to the north, where it was not difficult to relive the experience of the ancient commuter or day-tripper.

Whatever else it had achieved, the advent of the railways had killed Lichfield as a coaching city. The last long-distance coach, the Chester mail, was discontinued in 1838, and although coaches and omnibuses continued to operate after this time, it was usually to local towns or to a train station. Only with the invention of the combustion engine could the bus begin to stage a comeback. Motor buses were running to Whittington by 1916, though they were operating between Brownhills and Chasetown somewhat earlier. Initially bus services seem to have congregated in Market Square, later moving to the Friary and then (in the mid-1960s) to a new bus station on the Birmingham Road opposite City Station.

It remains questionable whether the canals and railways significantly increased manufacturing in the city, but they certainly attracted what traders there were to their environs. There were limeworks and a bonehouse adjacent

68 *Trent Valley Station, shortly after its opening in 1847. There were originally two stations at Trent Valley, one for the Trent Valley Railway and the other for the South Staffordshire. The two were combined in 1871, with a High Level and Low Level platform. The original building was preserved as the station master's house until its demolition in 1971.*

to the Wyrley & Essington Canal in the early 1800s, although the presence of the latter (described by the vicar of St Mary's as 'noisome and offensive') did not endear it to the inhabitants. The brewery industry, already well-established in the city, was irresistibly drawn to the railway. The Lichfield Brewery Co. built a brewery and a malthouse on Upper St John Street in 1873, where the Lichfield Aerated Water Co. also had premises. In the following year the City Brewery Co. opened a brewery and malthouse a little to the south of City Station, while the Trent Valley Brewery Co. built premises at Streethay in 1877. Signs of this once thriving industry can be still be found in the area today. The creation of the Trent Valley Trading Estate by the corporation in 1946 to encourage light engineering to the area is probably the last direct evidence of the railways' impact upon the development of the town. From this point onwards roads were to have more influence upon Lichfield's growth than railroads.

There remains to consider Darwin's third mode of transport, what he called 'the flying chariot'. Here, for once, Lichfield was given an early introduction to the latest technological advance. It was perhaps inevitable that, having waited two hundred years for the great man's prophecy to come true, two flying machines should arrive almost at once. The date was April 1910, less than ten years after the first powered flight, and Lichfield found itself on the flight path of the London to Manchester air race. The competition was sponsored by the *Daily Mail* newspaper, which offered a £10,000 prize to the first aviator able to cover the distance in less than 24 hours. Two pilots – an Englishman called Claude Graham-White and a Frenchman by the name of Louis Paulhan – immediately took up the challenge. Their arrival in Lichfield within a week of each other was no coincidence, for it was an early trick of the aviators to navigate by tracing the railway line. Not only were railway tracks easy to spot from the air, they were also unlikely to climb mountains. Therefore the most direct route from London to Didsbury was to follow the LNWR line through Rugby to Lichfield and Stafford. Graham-White attempted the flight twice, on both occasions electing to land near the level crossing at Hademore, before resting at the *George Hotel*. Both attempts were thwarted by bad weather. As for Paulhan, he too landed at Lichfield, near the Trent Valley railway station, and likewise spent the night at the *George*. The old coaching inn had suddenly discovered a new class of traveller!

Undoubtedly Paulhan's was the more professional attempt of the two, and a specially hired train, carrying friends, family and technical support, tracked his progress from below. (The railway company had nothing to fear of competition from the sky at this date.) Although he took off again at 4.00 o'clock in the morning, the *Lichfield Mercury* reported that a crowd of 3,000 well-wishers were present to see Paulhan begin the final leg of his journey. An hour and a half later, the Frenchman had landed at Didsbury and claimed his not inconsiderable prize. This was the last the city would see of flying machines for a while. Half a century later there would be Wellington bombers overhead, something that even Erasmus Darwin could not have predicted.

From way back in the coaching era Lichfield's transport requirements had always been in excess of what might be expected from a small town because of the presence of the army. Perhaps the most shocking example of the connection was the shooting of a young soldier, Private W. R. Davies, by the IRA on Lichfield City Station in June 1990. The link is evident enough in the formation of what later became the 1st battalion of the South Staffordshire Regiment. A plaque on the front of the *King's Head*, a coaching inn in Bird Street, commemorates the raising of Colonel Luke Lillingstone's

38th Regiment of Foot there in 1705. It was one of six new regiments ordered by parliament for Marlborough's campaign against the French, though Lillingstone's men did not in fact fight on that front. The army is one area where the tide of privatisation has run in the opposite direction from normal. In the 18th century the colonel himself would have been responsible for the provisions, uniform and pay of his men, for which he received a lump sum from the government. Their training needs alone would have taken up much of his time, for not long after formation Lillingstone's new recruits were described as 'a fragment of a regiment, from which no duty can be expected for some time'. Nevertheless, they did not have long to wait for active service; within weeks they were off to Ireland, to Spain and then to the West Indies. Indeed, in the first hundred years of its existence, the regiment spent sixty in the Caribbean, ten in America and most of the remainder in Ireland. The old adage about 'seeing the world' was not far wrong.

What was to become the 2nd battalion was not raised until 1793, but the period in between was hardly free from recruitment drives. Infantry volunteers signed up for regular drill and no active service, including one led by Peter Garrick, the actor's brother, and a Staffordshire Militia was formed in 1776 to counter the threat of a French invasion. These volunteers were subsequently to form the basis of the 80th Regiment of Foot, later the 2nd battalion of the South Staffords, raised by Lord Paget in 1793. A full account of the campaigns of these various units is beyond the scope of this book, but a visit to the cathedral, and especially to St Michael's chapel in the south transept (used as the regimental chapel since 1960), vividly illustrates how serving the British Empire could be both an exotic and a tragic experience. The campaigns of the 80th Regiment of Foot alone are represented by an Egyptian sphinx (for the First Sikh War), a line of African shields (for the Zulu War) and a mural tablet to commemorate the 352 officers and privates who died in Burma in 1852-3. Of the latter tropical disease accounted for all but ten of the casualties.

Not only was Lichfield the principal recruiting centre for the various Staffordshire militias and regiments, but it also served as their home base on the rare occasions that they were in England. The Staffordshire Yeomanry annually assembled in the town for their training week in June, an event that was not without its moments of friction. Notoriously in June 1884 a special performance of a Gilbert and Sullivan operetta at St James's Hall was reduced to anarchy when the soldiers attempted to storm the stage. This was, in a sense, perfect military training, but was here designed to gain entry to the actresses' dressing-rooms. Thwarted in their plan, high testosterone levels drove them out into the town instead, where fights broke out and Dr Johnson (his statue, that is) was assaulted.

For the regular soldiers, arriving back home meant a constant round of processions and cathedral services (dutifully and extensively described in the local press) and serious problems of accommodation. Billeting was over a wide area – as far as Stafford and Burton – until barracks were provided for the permanent staff and their families on the Birmingham Road in 1854. A visitor to Lichfield in 1855 remarked on the number of young soldiers he saw lounging about and looking 'as if they had had a little too much ale'. Whittington heath was in use as a training ground from the 1820s, but it was the army reforms of 1870, requiring each infantry regiment to establish a home depot and a reserve, that led to a more permanent use of the site. The Whittington barracks were built between 1877 and 1881, and the Staffordshire Regiment has been based there since that time.

69   *The grandstand of Whittington racecourse, now part of the Whittington golf club. In the late 1740s relations between the two political parties were so bad that rival race meetings were held for the Tories and Whigs. This, at least, prevented the hand-to-hand combat that occurred at the 1747 races. The meeting of 1769, when Eclipse, the greatest racehorse of the century, won the King's Plate, was perhaps Whittington's finest sporting hour.*

Military history ensured that Lichfield was rarely allowed to enjoy peaceful isolation from the outside world and, whatever the American visitor, Nathaniel Hawthorne, might have thought about Lichfeldians' innate suspicion of strangers, their presence was hardly unusual. French prisoners-of-war were a regular sight in the town throughout the 18th century. Those brought back from Guadeloupe in 1810 included black servants, and a number lie buried in St Michael's churchyard, a burial place shared (incidentally) with Trooper John Brown, whose trumpet sent the Light Brigade charging into the 'Valley of Death' at the Battle of Balaclava. In December 1797 Anna Seward records the presence of 80 French prisoners in the town:

> On their first arrival, and indeed long afterwards, they could not pass our
> streets without being brutally reviled by our populace … Though several

70 *A view of the city from St Michael's churchyard in the late 1840s. On the far left can be seen Christ Church, Leomonsley, and nearer the centre the tower of St Mary's church before its rebuilding in 1853. Parishioners of St Michael's reserved the right to pasture their sheep and cattle in the huge churchyard, despite the fact that a child was killed by a cow there in 1809.*

of the officers were men of graceful manners and enlightened minds, yet by no family of this city, mine and the Simpsons excepted, were they in the smallest degree noticed.

The Frenchmen did not have to endure Lichfield's cold shoulders for long. After ten months in the city they were being frog-marched to an even less welcoming jail in Liverpool.

Setting aside military and political differences, such continental connections were often enthusiastically embraced by the families in the close. In 1779, for example, Erasmus Darwin was employing a French officer on parole in the city to teach his children French, whilst a couple by the name of Latuffière were teaching their native language and manners at a boarding school in the close in the 1760s. On a less permanent note, in 1795 Miss Seward was

71 *A contemplative moment spent at the corner of the Friary and Bird Street. The classical portico was set up in 1937 to frame the entrance to the excavated ruins of the Franciscan Friary, though no one can say with certainty where the portico came from. At the time the Friary estate had a population of one, the tenant of a gardener's cottage.*

72 *The statue of Commander Edward John Smith, captain of the* Titanic, *in the Museum Gardens. Smith was a native of Hanley, but the memorial was erected in Lichfield 'as a convenient calling place for visitors travelling between London and Liverpool'. The sculptor was Kathleen Scott, the wife of the equally ill-fated polar explorer.*

lamenting the fall from grace of Mme le Chevalier d'Eton, who had fought (in disguise) in a number of campaigns in Germany and America, and was now reduced to demonstrating swordsmanship in the town at two shillings' admittance.

It was principally the advent of outsiders that reintroduced catholicism into the city after a 250-year hiatus. There was a Roman Catholic chapel above a baker's shop on the corner of Bore Street and Breadmarket Street in 1800, but the congregation was driven out by the heat from the ovens to a cooler and purpose-built chapel in Upper St John Street, which opened in 1803. The communicants consisted mainly of French prisoners and Irish refugees, who were making their way from Liverpool to London. Not all were simply passing through, however. A community of poor Irish people had settled around Sandford Street, supplemented by former navvies and miners. Their presence was hardly enough to turn Lichfield into a cosmopolitan society overnight, but perhaps it marks the beginnings of one.

CHAPTER TEN

Modern Times

The travel writers who passed through Lichfield towards the end of the 19th century were not, on the whole, very enthusiastic. 'Staid, sober and plodding ...' commented one, while the novelist, Henry James, called it 'stale without being really antique'. The general impression was of a place resting on its laurels, seemingly immune to the changes that were transforming the towns a few miles to the south. At a cursory glance the Ordnance Survey map of the city from 1882 does not look so different from John Snape's plan of a century before. The familiar dark cross of the cathedral remains, as does the grid of medieval streets below the Minster Pool, and the well known triangle of the Greenhill still draws the streets together before despatching them towards Burton and Tamworth. What Snape did not see were the two great curves of the railways – the South Staffordshire and the London & North Western – which were now sweeping past the city and intersecting at Trent Valley.

But closer scrutiny of the 1882 map shows that the city was indeed undergoing changes, subtler perhaps than in earlier centuries or in other places, but no less tangible for that. Near the railway the Trent Valley Brewery occupies a site almost as large as the cathedral, with a group of 12 cottages for the workers along the main road. The brewery was demolished in 1970, but it was an early precursor of industrial development along the Trent Valley Road.

To the north of the road the lay-out of fields serves to remind us that this was still a mainly rural area, although by the 1840s the arable fields to the west of the city were tending to concentrate on market gardening. The names on the map – Townfield cottages, Gaiafields, Brown's Fields, Leyfield cottage – recall the great open fields and common land where medieval townsfolk sowed their crops and grazed their cattle, but enclosure had long since removed that right and fenced in the land. The presence of two cattle markets in the town itself also reflects the new intensity of livestock production. One smithfield stood behind the *Swan Hotel*, and another on Church Street, though on some days they diversified into wool and dairy produce. But even here Lichfield struggled to maintain such trade in the long term. The market at the *Swan* closed in 1906, while Winterton's moved their auction out to Fradley in 1988.

Moving further north the two houses at Stowe that had once entertained Johnson and Boswell still stood as testimony to Georgian days. Here too the map conceals considerable changes in ownership and use. Stowe House had seen a succession of owners and tenants in the years since Elizabeth Aston had lived there, the most notable of whom was probably the banker, Richard Greene, who occupied it with his family and eight servants in the 1840s and 1850s. Greene's grandfather was the Richard Greene who had single-handedly created Lichfield's first museum, and the grandson followed in the family tradition, owning an extensive collection of rare books and paintings. But Greene's comfortable lifestyle came to an abrupt end in 1856 when his bank collapsed with liabilities of £75,000. The house and contents (lock, stock and wine cellar) were sold and so Stowe House passed through another sequence of hands before being taken over by the city council in 1945. Initially redesigned to accommodate a nurses' home, it became a management training centre in 1969. As for Stowe Hill, tucked away behind its shield of trees, it too saw a variety of owners – wealthy widows and Black Country ironmaster – before land for building was carved out of its 19 acres in the mid-1950s.

Turning south-west along the straight line of Stowe Pool (its corrected geometry courtesy of the South Staffordshire Waterworks) we enter Gaia. Much of Gaia had been laid out for market gardens by the 1880s, filling the area between Prince Rupert's Mound and the cathedral close, until it reached Beacon Street. On the far side of the street was another substantial house that John Snape would not have seen. Beacon Place, first built in the late 18th century, had grown in size and stature to become 'one of the best houses in the neighbourhood', with an estate not far short of 100 acres. The gift of an acre or so of the grounds by Richard Hinkley and his wife in 1847 for a new church – Christ Church – hardly interrupted its expansion, though it gave the Hinkley family somewhere to go for burial. Ellen Jane Hinkley had much need of monuments, and her story is one of the sadder tales of 19th-century Lichfield. By the time she married Richard Hinkley she had already been widowed twice, and would indeed outlive her third husband as well.

73 *An aerial view of the south of the city. The area between Birmingham Road (opened in 1955) and Wade Street has been the focus of redevelopment for 40 years. By the time of this 1970 photograph the Bakers Lane shopping centre and car park had been completed, but the future civic hall site remained empty. Further commercial expansion is now planned for the bus station area.*

Her first marriage to William Robinson, a prebendary of the cathedral (her father was the dean), was especially tragic. William Robinson died of consumption in 1812 while still a young man, leaving his wife and two daughters. Within two years the two daughters were dead too, one the victim of consumption, the other from burns when her nightdress caught fire. As such the deaths reflect the two chief dangers of life in the 19th-century town, but the monument that commemorates them was far from typical.

The memorial to Marianne and Ellen Jane Robinson in the south choir aisle of the cathedral is so unlike any other that it has attracted attention ever since its erection in 1817, and even before that when it was exhibited at the Royal Academy. Francis Chantrey's 'Sleeping Children' has remained a perennial favourite on the postcard rack since ever there were souvenirs to buy, the simple marble figures (the younger with snowdrops in her hand) capturing the imagination more than any recumbent bishop. Artistically the sculpture leans towards the sentimentality of the Victorians, when 'fallen asleep' would become a familiar graveyard inscription. But this was 1817, when simple naturalism was a rare feature of church monuments, and the two little girls in white Carrara marble still surprise the visitor. The form of the memorial was, by all accounts, the idea of Mrs Robinson herself, and having 'consigned their resemblances to the sanctuary' (as the inscription goes) she carried such simple sorrows through to the death of her second husband and of her son, whom she buried in the new churchyard behind Beacon Place. The house itself stood until 1964, when it was purchased by the city council and knocked down. A private developer built houses on part of the grounds, while the rest was incorporated into the recreation grounds which still recall its name.

There is one more estate to consider, butting up against the city streets on the west as it had for 600 years. The poor friars who had owned the Friary before the Reformation had been replaced by less penurious politicians, but the terms of the lease did not allow its conversion into a private estate like its neighbours. It remained, much as it had after the Tudor demolition crews had moved out, a collection of ancient buildings encircling the ground vacated by the church and cloisters. If it had been a political act to dissolve the Friary, it was the act of another politician to sweep it away for good. Sir Richard Cooper, MP for Walsall, handed over the land for redevelopment in 1920. The main intention was to relieve traffic congestion by cutting a new road from Bird Street to the Walsall and Birmingham roads. In the words of a city alderman, the gift 'let daylight into Lichfield'; the reality was to let more cars in. In the long run, however, the new road encouraged a tentative expansion of housing westwards. The site of the Friary itself was now irrevocably cut in two, but the city showed itself unwilling to dispose of its past too wilfully. The southern range of buildings (now shared between the public library and archives and Lichfield College) was initially handed over to a private school for girls. Across the road, after the site of the church had been excavated, a grand and seemingly pointless portico was erected in 1937, showing that neo-classical tastes had not entirely deserted the city fathers.

If we move into the town centre, the 1882 map shows changes here too, albeit that continuity remained the dominant force. A major development, seen in the number of schools now dotted across the map, was in the extended provision of education. School building boomed in the Victorian town. Unlike its near neighbours, Lichfield had no need of Forster's Education Act of 1870, there being already sufficient school places for the city's children. But it also meant that the Church of England was by far the dominant force.

The grammar school, of course, still occupied its traditional site on St John Street, but there was little other than the buildings to connect it with its golden age of Addison and Johnson. Indeed, there were times in the 19th century when the school did not have any pupils at all. Much of this failure must be placed at the door of the headmaster, Cowperthwaite Smith, who held the post for 36 years from 1813. Despite the conditions attached to his salary (funded by the Conduit Lands Trust) that 'he conducts himself with sobriety of Life and Conversation and with a Diligence and Attention to the duties of his office', Smith's diligence hardly extended beyond the use of the cane, and only with his retirement (no doubt weary from his exertions) could the school embark on long needed reconstruction. New buildings went up in 1850, but the need for accommodation for boarders eventually sent it to Borrowcop Hill in 1903, where it remains, now as part of the state comprehensive system.

Something of an educational quarter had grown up in this part of the town by the end of the 19th century. Next to the grammar school a high school for girls had taken over Yeomanry House by 1896, forming the basis of what would one day become Friary Grange, and along Frog Lane yet another school (founded in 1809 in a converted barn) catered for boys aged between six and twelve. Conversion would not have needed to be too radical, since the school operated on the 'monitorial' system, one teacher delivering all the education necessary to a single classroom, with the help of older pupils acting as monitors. (Another converted barn in Quoniams Lane gave similar schooling to girls.) Cheap to run, the Frog Lane school could therefore afford to provide an annual pair of shoes to the boys and a regular haircut, though this free styling was later (as the hair itself) cut to save money. Given the dearth of free education in the town the national school was understandably popular, with an average of 100 pupils throughout the century. Despite the constricted site it was almost the last school to vacate the city centre, moving out to Nether Stowe (along with its 350 children) in 1964.

By the Victorian era it was recognised that education was an important tool in combating anti-social behaviour, and Lichfield's low crime rate no doubt encouraged neighbouring authorities to place their more difficult youngsters there. An 'industrial school' for girls (what we would now call a remand home) was built by the county council on Wissage Lane in 1889, its secure site reflected in the fact that it was later used as an isolation hospital. The boroughs of Burton, West Bromwich and Walsall similarly funded a truant school for boys at the north end of Beacon Street four years later.

Efforts to create an environment in which adults could learn and train were far less successful. The Lichfield Working Men's Association, which met in Tamworth Street, had begun well enough in the 1830s, with over 350 men learning to read, write and sing, but it fell away by the closing years of the century. The establishment of a more formal School of Art, on the corner of Dam Street and Pool Walk, was doubtless a factor in its decline, and the new art school later expanded to include scientific and technical instruction, while the numbers signing up for watercolours declined. Given the problems faced by the public library, the idea of siting another place of education next to the Minster Pool would appear to be foolhardy, and sure enough the building was in trouble by 1950: subsidence was always ready to move in when subsidies moved out. Like the library, the School of Art found a drier refuge in the Friary.

Similarly chequered was Lichfield's great theatrical tradition (or lack of one). When we last visited the Theatre Royal (three chapters ago) it was in process of demolition. Its successor, built on the same site, was St James's Hall, which offered entertainment that was nothing if not varied. In a typical month in 1877 the hall staged a lecture called 'Reminiscences of the Crimea', a concert by Emily Lloyd and a show by 'Matthews' Champion Coloured Comedians'. It also hosted cosmoramas and other forms of moving pictures, which by 1910 were on celluloid. The series of changes that now overtook the Bore Street premises was not unusual for entertainment venues, but they were not helped either by recurrent fires or the difficulty in attracting a sufficiently large customer base. In 1912 St James's Hall had become the

74   *The Bower procession passing the cathedral in 1966. Stebbing Shaw comments that 'to increase their amusement there were displayed a variety of other exhibitions adapted to the taste of those times, such as bear and bull baitings, interludes, flying-chain, legerdemain practitioners and wild beasts.' The bower queen was added to this motley list in 1930.*

Palladium cinema, only to be sold and converted once more in 1936, when Lichfeldians picked up a taste for what was then touted as the 'luxury cinema'. By then the Lido (as it was now called) had competition from a rival house – the Regal – in Tamworth Street. The Regal had the advantage of being purpose-built, and (from the 1940s) of being part of a major chain. This is at least part of the explanation for why the Lido had failed by 1949 and the Regal survived until 1974, though both would ultimately find themselves on the primrose path to disuse, bingo hall and supermarket conversion. The opening of the Civic Hall in Wade Street in the same year at least spared Lichfield the ignominy of having nowhere to show and see films.

So stood the city as the Victorian age drew to its close. It was, on the whole, a quiet place, but it was on the threshold of a much noisier century. A town with such strong military connections as Lichfield knew more than most that war can change the direction of life, and those which arrived in 1914 and 1939 could hardly fail to do so. The creation of St Michael's chapel in the south transept of the cathedral as a memorial to the soldiers who died in the First World War illustrates the complex and curious link between combat and Christianity, and a war that claimed around 20,000 men in the Staffordshire regiments was bound to leave its mark on the county. A military ward was added to the cottage hospital at Hammerwich and Beacon House was taken over by the War Department as offices. Nearby, a First World War gun was added to other assorted memorials in the Museum Gardens, until (ironically) it became part of the scrap metal collecting for the next war. The end of hostilities was celebrated in style by a city that was much practised in such revelries. (The conclusion of the Crimean War had been marked in similar fashion in 1856.) A weekend in July 1919 was set aside for a torchlight procession, athletics on the recreation grounds and dancing in the Museum Grounds. There were, however, some mutterings of disapproval at the official announcement of corporation cost cutting:

> Citizens are cordially requested to display Flags and Decorations during the day and to illuminate their houses at dusk. The council will not undertake any public decorations.

Such complaints were addressed by the formal laying-out of a War Memorial Garden next to Minster Pool in 1920.

If the Great War touched Lichfield only peripherally, the impact of the Second World War was much more direct. For one thing the house building programme, stimulated by Lloyd George's call for 'homes for heroes', came to a grinding halt, as did the slum clearance scheme centred upon Wade Street and Sandford Street. Not all building work ceased, however. The fire which broke out in the Lido cinema in November 1942 might easily have spelt the end of its chequered career, but because of the presence of large numbers of servicemen in the town, as well as the general issue of morale, this could not be allowed to happen. Within eight months it had re-opened for business. As before, the war meant the requisitioning of buildings by the War Office: the Royal Army Service Corps took over Beacon House, a British Restaurant operated out of the Methodist Hall in Tamworth Street, and Stowe House was handed over to Belmont School, evacuated from the town of Hassocks in Sussex. Evacuees were a common site in Lichfield at this time. Many were children from Birmingham and West Bromwich, but the numbers also included Jewish tailors from the east end of London, who evidently did not find it easy to ply their trade successfully in this new environment. The pressure to accommodate this new influx of residents allowed the council to continue some of its house building (mainly on the new Ponesfield estate), but priority here was given to workers at RAF Alrewas, where there were almost 2,000 ground and air crew by the middle of 1942.

For a place the size of Lichfield evacuees swelled the population considerably: by 1941 there were over 2,000 living in the city. But arriving evacuees who imagined that they were escaping from the front line were to be rudely awakened. Lichfield was too close to centres of industry and to army and airforce bases to be spared completely. The Luftwaffe did not call as often as it did on Birmingham, but still there was damage enough (390 houses) and three deaths.

The aerodrome at Fradley in Alrewas was constructed in 1939-40, originally as a maintenance unit for modifying Hurricanes, but by April 1941 it had been taken over by the RAF and was accommodating Wellington bombers as well. By the following year the 50 Wellingtons were becoming a familiar sight in the skies over the city as they began their long-haul raids on Hamburg and Dresden. Down on the ground the city got used to hearing colonial accents in the bars. Of the 462 air crew there were 180 Australians, 26 New Zealanders and 24 Canadians. There were American accents too, for Whittington barracks had become the US Army's 10th Reinforcement Depot by 1944. What went on in the guardhouses there put the name of Lichfield into the headlines of newspapers on both sides of the Atlantic in 1946, when

75 *The mayor of Lichfield, Councillor Thomas Moseley, presenting a casket to Colonel James A. Kilian at a ceremony in the Guildhall in December 1944 to honour the presence of the US Army. Colonel Kilian's command was not so well appreciated down at the barracks.*

nine guards faced trial for 'their cruel and inhuman disciplinary treatment of stockade prisoners during the winter of 1944-5'. American prisoners, many of whom were black, were subjected to solitary confinement in unlit and insanitary cells and deprivation of food that almost amounted to starvation. The courts martial, held in London, found the guards guilty, but also concluded that they were 'only obeying orders'. Although he was not in the dock himself, it was the commandant of the base, Colonel James A. Kilian, who faced the worst criticism for 'aiding, authorizing and abetting' the cruelties. In the wake of the trials General Eisenhower ordered a wide-ranging investigation into disciplinary procedures at US Army bases.

Once the loose ends of the war were tied up Lichfield could resume its reconstruction, but with renewed urgency. The need to diversify and deepen the town's employment base was a strong driving force in the immediate post-war period. Spurred on by the Board of Trade, in 1946 the corporation purchased Trent Valley House, a large Victorian mansion lying between the railway and Trent Valley Road, and turned the grounds into the city's first industrial estate. The intention was to attract light industry to the town, and the firms based there in the 1950s (often secondary units of parent companies in Birmingham and the Black Country, tempted across the boundary by cheap rents and government grants) were making predominantly electrical and dairy equipment, furniture and plastics. GKN opened an electrical components factory there in 1949. The estate was extended in the early 1960s, and again a decade later. From the 1940s onwards we can no longer consider the history of Lichfield in isolation from the surrounding region. All the towns, new and old, in close proximity to the West Midlands were required to take their fair share of overspill population, and (if that was not to create a transportation nightmare) jobs had to move with them. County development plans drove the policy forward from the 1950s through to the 1990s, though by the end of the century the Lichfield District Local Plan (1994) was heeding the Secretary of State's recommendation that there should be limits to headlong expansion, if only to preserve the green belt. By then the old airfield at Fradley represented the one last area for continued expansion.

It was not difficult to encourage people to live in the city – Lichfield remained and remains an attractive place to live – but to build up an industrial or even a post-industrial economy was another matter. Towns do not change their spots overnight. In Georgian times Lichfield was a place renowned for its service sector, and the industrial revolution that passed it by in the 18th century was not about to call a second time. In 1950 the service industries accounted for 64.6 per cent of employment in the city, as opposed to 32.5 per cent in manufacturing. By the late 1980s, despite the new industrial estates, these proportions had hardly altered: 66 per cent in services and 34 per cent in manufacturing. Nor was the provision of jobs equally divided between male and female. Fostering an industrial sector from scratch revealed a severe skills shortage among males. However, women workers there were in larger numbers, especially in the coalfields which had always provided few opportunities for females. By the 1960s firms such as the Lichfield City Laundry were being forced to bus in women workers from Brownhills, Hednesford and Rugeley.

By the 1970s what jobs there were in the service and manufacturing sectors did not begin to meet the needs of an expanded population. Half of the residents were travelling out of the city to work. The electrification of what was now called the Cross City line in the late 1980s helped to soak up some of this increased commuter movement, but the roads have (as always in Lichfield) borne the heaviest burden. The creation of the Birmingham Road in the mid-'50s and the Western Relief Road at the end of the decade were early attempts to cope with this increasing demand. The Birmingham Northern Relief Road at the end of the century followed in this tradition.

The growth in population and housing was most marked in the 1970s and 1980s, especially for a place that had for centuries hardly edged above 3,000 people. By 1951 the total had passed 10,000, and by 1991 it exceeded 28,000. Compared with national averages the 1981 census showed a greater preponderance of residents in their late 20s and 30s, reflecting the population drift of the '70s, but unlike surrounding areas the resident population remained almost exclusively white, containing only a third of the national average for people not born in the UK. The creation of new housing was a major factor in Lichfield's development in the post-war period, changing the map significantly in the outlying areas. The Boley Park development to the east of the city was undoubtedly the biggest of these, its 2,000 houses making it one of the largest private estates in Europe. Alongside it a new industrial park was initiated in 1981, with a major new road to link it to the Eastern By-pass and Eastern Avenue. The chosen name – Cappers Lane – recalled the far-off time when cappers were the most numerous manufacturers in the city. That was some 400 years ago.

The increased mobility offered by the car, whether for shops, employment or entertainment, has made it increasingly difficult for a small town to offer the full range of facilities that once came as standard. In a sense Lichfield in the 20th century was continuing to reap the bitter harvest sowed by the early medieval dispersal of Staffordshire as a dis-unitary authority. Such difficulties can be instanced in each of these three areas. In terms of the arts the creation of a music and later a more general arts festival in the early 1980s (largely originating in the cathedral) showed that the city could be the successful host of such occasional events. Offering artistic excellence on a wet November night was another matter. In 1970 the city council took over the former post office in Bird Street (opened in 1905) as an arts centre, and converted it into gallery space and a cafe. The forced closure of the museum across the road might have been taken as a harbinger of doom for the enterprise, but it was not. Nevertheless, the subsidence which had undermined so many educational foundations in the city was not to be denied, and in February 1994 the Bird

76   *The Bakers Lane shopping precinct, designed by Shingler & Risdon of London. The lane stands on the line of a medieval street (once known as Pease Porridge Lane). The houses along Bakers Lane in Victorian times were among the city's worst and were condemned in 1891.*

Street centre too was obliged to close. From this point onwards the arts became an unedifying spectacle of political football between the city's two main political parties. In 1997 the Labour council unveiled plans for a £1.7 million plan to redevelop the centre, with a controversial steel-and-glass creation by the Dutch architect, Erick van Egeraat. This scheme was ditched by the Conservatives after the 1999 local elections, and replaced by an even grander (and more costly) proposal to redevelop the Civic Hall. The latter project (inevitably opposed by the Labour group) finally went ahead in 2001, dovetailing into a new commercial redevelopment on Levetts Square.

A shopping precinct centred on Bakers Lane was created in the early 1960s, but by 1994 (when the centre was showing the signs of tiredness felt by all such precincts) it was still generally recognised that Lichfield was 'under-shopped', lacking any supermarket or department store in the city centre. Plans to address this problem were being considered from as far back as 1980, wanting only for a developer. Inevitably that interest came from outside the area, and a London-based company – St Mary's Property Investments – found the necessary capital for the project to begin in the

77 *Sir Francis Chantrey's 'Sleeping Children' in the south choir aisle of the cathedral. Chantrey was the most famous sculptor of his age, and this became his most popular work, a pleasing antidote to the grandiose funerary monuments then in vogue. Chantrey's inspiration came from the memorial to Penelope, daughter of Sir Brooke Boothby, in Ashbourne church.*

mid-1990s. The Three Spires Shopping Centre opened in 1995-6 at a cost of £9 million, with the now mandatory multi-storey car park, and a logo that made the cathedral spires curiously resemble the pyramids of Giza. In 2000 the same company embarked on a major redevelopment of Levetts Square.

It was inevitable that all these developments would take place in the area around Bakers Lane, Wade Street and Frog Lane, the least sensitive in terms of preservation of buildings, and where sub-standard housing had been cleared away in the 1930s. The glut of post-war building in these streets still comes as something of a shock to the visitor emerging from the well-preserved area to the north. Although included in the overall conservation area strategy of 1970, it contained only one listed property, the congregational chapel of 1812. It does, however, serve to illustrate the dilemma faced by a city that welcomes visitors who live in its past (as a whole the district had 2,000 jobs in tourism in the mid-'90s) and residents who live in its present. Nevertheless,

78   *The Court of Array, as photographed by Sir Benjamin Stone in 1908. The ceremony
traditionally took place at Greenhill on the morning of the Whitsun fair, attended by the high
constables and ten representatives of the wards, morris dancers and a fool 'fantastically arrayed'.
It is now held in the Guildhall.*

given the increasing importance of tourism to the British economy, it is a
problem that every other town in the Midlands would probably wish was
theirs.

Lichfield's early prominence as an ecclesiastical centre had given it
political and legal significance that was probably disproportionate to its
true status and importance. A town of 6,000 in the 1850s could hardly be
called a 'rotten borough', but when parliament began to consider a more
equitable redistribution of power it would do the city no favours. In terms of
national representation, Lichfield had traditionally returned two members to
Westminster. Disraeli's reform act of 1867 reduced this to one, and in 1885
the city was merged into a much larger constituency, covering much of south-
east Staffordshire. From 1983 the seat was known as Mid-Staffordshire.

Changes in local government were, if anything, even more dramatic.
When the corporation members refused to cooperate with the Municipal

79 *Lichfield's other example of living tradition – the Sheriff's Ride – in September 1938. The charter of Charles II specified that 'the sheriff should on the feast of the nativity of the blessed Virgin Mary yearly, under pain of fine and amerciament, perambulate the boundaries of the city and country of Lichfield and the precincts thereof'. It is, however, much quicker to cover the 16 miles on a horse.*

Commissioners in 1835 they shrewdly recognised that visitors from London with maps and plans do not generally augur well. In fact the Municipal Corporations Act of that year only served to place the council on a more secure footing, with a mayor and 18 elected councillors. But where the officials of 1885 trod softly, their successors were not so polite. Since Queen Mary's charter of 1553 Lichfield had enjoyed the unusual status of 'city and county'; the Local Government Act of 1888 took a sharp axe to this anomaly. From this point onwards Lichfield was formally reunited with the county of Staffordshire, and with the loss of county status also had to relinquish its coroner. Another Local Government Act in 1972 went further still, removing Lichfield's power of self-government and uniting the city and the rural district councils into a single entity – Lichfield District Council – with offices in St John Street. Luckily for Lichfield's self-esteem this step was partly reversed in 1980 with the establishment of a parish council, which in turn petitioned the Queen for the restoration of city status. This was granted by letters patent in November 1980.

80 *The Museum Gardens in 1955. The docile lions were donated by Sir Richard Cooper in the 1880s to supplement Chancellor Law's fountain, while the statue of Edward VII was presented by Robert Bridgeman in 1908. The combination of Beacon Park, Museum Gardens and Minster Pool has created a green corridor across the centre of the city.*

The upshot of all these changes was complex and somewhat confusing. For one thing, Lichfield was in the unusual position of having been granted city status twice; for another, it was one of only six places in England to be both a city and a parish, and (with a population of almost 30,000) was the largest of them. But there was, and is, the nagging suspicion that the regalia of civic pride had replaced real local control. A full analysis of the responsibilities of these three tiers of local government is beyond the scope of this book, and undoubtedly a matter of some bewilderment to the city's inhabitants. The position of Lichfield's three weekly markets is probably the best example. The Saturday market is operated by the district council, while the city council runs the Tuesday market. The Friday market, on the other hand, is managed by the district council on behalf of the city, the costs being split between the two bodies.

So stood Johnson's 'city of philosophers' as it entered its third millennium. It had come a long way from dark woods and cattle raiders, holy wells and pilgrims, but there was more than a thread of continuity running through the story. We should allow the doctor the final word, if only because he would have insisted on it in his lifetime. What Johnson said (in Latin) of the stream that ran from Stowe Pool past the Church of St Chad is equally true of the history of Lichfield itself, and indeed of all history:

Hard axes have now destroyed those ancient shades;
The pool lies naked, even to distant eyes.
But the water, never tiring, still runs on
In the same channel, sometimes hidden,
Sometimes visible, but ever flowing.

Bibliography

General

Greenslade, M.W., ed., *A History of the County of Stafford*, Vol 14 (Lichfield) (Oxford, 1990)

Godwin, John, *Lichfield Miscellany* (Lichfield, 1978)

Gould, J., *Lichfield Archaeology and Development* (Birmingham, 1976)

Harper, Rob, *Lichfield City Conservation Area Document. A Guide to the Buildings and Features of Historic Interest in Lichfield Conservation* Area (Lichfield, 1987)

Harwood, Thomas, *The History and Antiquities of the Church and City of Lichfield* (Gloucester, 1806)

James, Ralph, *Lichfield Then and Now* (Lichfield, 1988)

Laithwaite, Percy, *The History of the Conduit Lands Trust 1546 to 1946* (Lichfield, 1947)

Plot, Robert, *A Natural History of Staffordshire* (Oxford, 1686)

Shaw, Stebbing, *The History and Antiquities of Staffordshire* (1798, 1801, reprinted Wakefield, 1976)

Thorpe, H., 'Lichfield: A Study of its Growth and Function', SHC (1950-1), 137-211

Chapter 1: Beside the Grey Wood

Carver, M.O.H., 'The Archaeology of Early Lichfield: An Inventory and Some Recent Results', *T.S.S.A.H.S.*, 22, 1-12

Gelling, Margaret, *The West Midlands in the Early Middle Ages*, Leicester UP, 1992

Gould, J., 'Lichfield – Ecclesiastical Origins' in *In Search of Cult: Archaeological Investigations in Honour of Philip Rahtz* (Woodbridge, 1993), pp.101-4

Johnson, Douglas, '"Lichfield" and "St Amphibalus": The Story of a Legend', *T.S.S.A.H.S.*, 28, 1-13

Palliser, D.M., 'A Thousand Years of Staffordshire: Man and the Landscape 913-1973', *North Staffordshire Journal of Field Studies*, 14, 21-33

Studd, Robin, 'Pre-Conquest Lichfield', *T.S.S.A.H.S.*, 22, 24-34

Vleeskruyer, R., ed., *The Life of St Chad: An Old English Homily*, Amsterdam, 1953

Whiston, J.W., 'Ryknild Street from Wall to Streethay, Staffs', *T.S.S.A.H.S.*, 19, 1-4

Chapter 2: Lichfield New Town

Bassett, S.R., 'Medieval Lichfield: A Topographical Review', *T.S.S.A.H.S.*, 22, 93-121

Crosby, A.G., 'Lichfield Kersey in the Early Sixteenth Century: Some References in Manx Correspondence', *T.S.S.A.H.S.*, 32, 85-6

Gould, J., 'Finds of Medieval Leather and Pottery from Near Minster Pool, Lichfield, Staffs', *T.S.S.A.H.S.*, 14, 51-60

Isaac, J., 'Two Medieval Accounts for the Town of Lichfield', *T.S.S.A.H.S.*, 18, 59-67

Kettle, A.J., 'City and Close: Lichfield in the Century before the Reformation', in Barron C. M. and Harper-Bill, C. (eds.), *The Church in Pre-Reformation Society* (Woodbridge, 1985), pp. 158-69

Palliser, D.M. and Pinnock, A.C., 'The Markets of Medieval Staffordshire', *North Staffordshire Journal of Field Studies*, 11, 49-63

Rosser, A. G., 'The Town and Guild of Lichfield in the Late Middle Ages', *T.S.S.A.H.S.*, 27, 39-47

Savage, H.E., ed., 'The Great Register of Lichfield Cathedral', *SHC* (1924), pp. 219-20 and 141-3

Slater, T.R., 'The Topography and Planning of Medieval Lichfield: A Critique', *T.S.S.A.H.S.*, 26, 11-35

Taylor, C.C., 'The Origins of Lichfield, Staffs', *T.S.S.A.H.S.*, 10, 43-52

Tringham, N.K., 'Five Church Courts at Lichfield in 1326', *T.S.S.A.H.S.*, 32, 79-82

Gould, J., 'The 12th-Century Water Supply to Lichfield Close', *Antiquaries Journal*, 56, 73-9

Chapter 3: Reforming Zeal

Anderson, M., 'Some Early Churchwardens' Accounts of Lichfield St Michael's', *T.S.S.A.H.S.*, 7, 11-20

Greenslade, M.W., ed., *A History of the County of Stafford*, Vol. III (Oxford, 1970)

Harrison, C.J., 'Lichfield from the Reformation to the Civil War', *T.S.S.A.H.S.*, 22, 122-29

Heath, P., 'Staffordshire Towns and the Reformation,' *North Staffordshire Journal of Field Studies*, 19, 1-21

Lehmberg, Stanford E., *The Reformation of Cathedrals* (Princeton, New Jersey, 1988)

O'Day, R., 'Cumulative Debt: The Bishops of Coventry and Lichfield and their Economic Problems', *Midland History*, 3, 77-93

Nichols, J., *Progresses and Public Processions of Queen Elizabeth* (London, 1823), Vol.1, pp. 529-31

'Star Chamber Proceedings. Henry VIII and Edward VI', *SHC* (1910), 137-8, 194-6

Vaisey, D.G., 'Probate Inventories of Lichfield and District 1568-1680', *SHC* (4th Series), 5

Wrottesley, F.J., 'The Inventory of Church Goods and Ornaments Taken in Staffordshire in 6E.VI. (1552)', *SHC* (2nd Series), 6, 177-8

Chapter 4: The Bloody City of Lichfield

Clayton, Howard, *Loyal and Ancient City. The Civil War in Lichfield* (Lichfield, n.d.)

Johnson, D.A. and Vaisey, D.G., *Staffordshire and the Great Rebellion* (Stafford, 1964)

Pennington, D.H. and Roots, I.A., 'The Committee at Stafford 1643-1645', *SHC* (4th Series), 1

Chapter 5: A Society of Antiquaries

Frew, J.M., 'Cathedral Improvement: James Wyatt at Lichfield Cathedral 1787 – 92', *T.S.S.A.H.S.*, 19, 33-45

Johnson, D., '"Mr. Greene's MSS"': Richard Greene's Notes on the History of Lichfield', *T.S.S.A.H.S.*, 30, 64-69

Josten, C.H., ed., *Elias Ashmole* (Oxford, 1966), 5 vols

Josten, C.H., 'Elias Ashmole and the 1685 Lichfield Election: An Unpublished Episode', *SHC* (1950-1), 213-227

Kendall, Alan, *David Garrick. A Biography* (London, 1985)

Kettle, Ann J., 'Lichfield Races', *T.S.S.A.H.S.*, 6, 39-44

Marr, Peter, 'John Alcock (1715-1806), Vicar Choral and Organist at Lichfield Cathedral: A Frustrated Reformer', *T.S.S.A.H.S.*, 21, 25–33

Marston, F., 'The "Hate House", Lichfield, Staffs. And Rev. Dr. James Falconer', *T.S.S.A.H.S.*, 12, 49-53

Lockett, R.B., 'Joseph Potter: Cathedral Architect at Lichfield 1794-1842', *T.S.S.A.H.S.*, 21, 34–47

Parnaby, R., 'Murals Found in a Bird Street Shop', *T.S.S.A.H.S.*, 2, 53

Smith, Helen R., *David Garrick* (British Library Monographs, 1979)

'The Staffordshire Hearth Tax', *SHC* (1912), pp. 239-40 (close); (1936), pp. 143-77 (city)

Tringham, N.J., 'Bishop's Palace, Lichfield Cathedral Close: Its Construction 1686-87', *T.S.S.A.H.S.*, 27, 57-63

Tringham, N.J., 'Two Seventeenth-Century Surveys of Lichfield Cathedral Close', *T.S.S.A.H.S.*, 25, 35-49

Tringham, N.J., 'Bishop's Palace, Lichfield Cathedral Close: Its Construction 1686-87', *T.S.S.A.H.S.*, 27, 57-63

Chapter 6: A City of Philosophers

Bate, Walter Jackson, *Samuel Johnson* (London, 1978)

Clayton, Howard, *Coaching City* (Bala, Wales, 1970)

Greene, D., 'Samuel Johnson's Staffordshire', *Staffordshire Studies*, 1, 1-21

Hopkins, Mary Alden, *Dr Johnson's Lichfield* (New York, 1952)

Kettle, A.J., 'The Struggle for the Lichfield Interest 1747-68', *SHC* (1970), 115-35

Lane, Margaret, *Samuel Johnson and his World* (London, 1975)

Phillips, A.D.M. and Turton, B.J., 'The Turnpike Network of Staffordshire, 1700-1840: An Introduction and a Handlist of Turnpike Acts', *SHC* (1988), 61-118

Rowlands, M.B., 'Industry and Social Change in Staffordshire 1660-1760. A Study of Probate and Other Records of Tradesmen', *T.S.S.A.H.S.*, 9, 37-58

Shaw, John, *The Old Pubs of Lichfield* (Lichfield, 2001)

Sherbo, Arthur, ed., *William Shaw: Memoirs of the Life and Writings of the Late Dr Samuel Johnson. Hesther Lynch Piozzi: Anecdotes of the Late Samuel Johnson* (London, 1974)

Speck, S.A., 'Staffordshire in the Reign of Queen Anne', *Staffordshire Studies*, 4, 21-34

Staffordshire General and Commercial Directory (1818)

Thomas, A.L., 'Geographical Aspects of the Development of Transport etc in North Staffordshire during the Eighteenth Century', *SHC* (1934), 1-157

Chapter 7: Close Families

Brewer, John, *The Pleasures of the Imagination. English Culture in the Eighteenth Century* (London, 1997)

Clarke, Desmond, *The Ingenious Mr Edgeworth* (London, 1965)

King-Hele, Desmond, *Doctor of Revolution. The Life and Genius of Erasmus Darwin* (London, 1977)

King-Hele, Desmond, ed., *The Letters of Erasmus Darwin* (Cambridge, 1981)

Lucas, E.V., *A Swan and her Friends* (London, 1907)

McNeil, Maureen, *Under the Banner of Science. Erasmus Darwin and his Age* (Manchester, 1987)

Pearson, Hesketh, *The Swan of Lichfield. A Selection from the Correspondence of Anna Seward* (London, 1936)

Tringham, N.J., 'An Early Eighteenth-Century Description of Lichfield Cathedral', *T.S.S.A.H.S.*, 28, 55-63

Chapter 8: A Tale of Two Cities

Clayton, Howard, *Cathedral City. A Look at Victorian Lichfield* (Lichfield, 1981)

Hornsey, Brian, *Ninety Years of Cinema in Lichfield* (Stamford, 1992)

Chapter 9: Trains and Boats and Planes

Christiansen, Rex, *A Regional History of the Railways of Great Britain*, Vol. 7 (Trowbridge, Wiltshire, 1973)

Hadfield, Charles, *The Canals of the East Midlands* (Newton Abbot, 1966)

Gould, J., 'The Lichfield Canal and the Wychnor Ironworks', *T.S.S.A.H.S.*, 23, 109-17

Moore, D.A., *Restoring the Lichfield Canal* (The Lichfield & Hatherton Restoration Trust, 1992)

Sell, A.P.F., 'George Burder and the Lichfield Dissenters', *T.S.S.A.H.S.*, 13, 52-60 (Ashbourne, 1896)

Lichfield Garrison. Standing Orders (Lichfield, 1895)

Staffordshire Advertiser, *The Military Forces of Staffordshire in the Nine-teenth Century* (1901)

Vale, Col. W.L., *History of the South Staffordshire Regiment* (Aldershot, 1969)

Chapter 10: Modern Times

Clayton, Howard and Simmons, Kathleen, eds., *Lichfield in Old Photographs* (Stroud, Gloucestershire, 1994)

Giddings, Malcolm L., Bomber Base. *A History of the Royal Air Force Lichfield and Church Broughton*

Gieck, Jack, Lichfield. *The U.S. Army on Trial* (Akron, Ohio, 1997)

Keyte, Owen, *The Annals of a Century: Bridgeman's of Lichfield 1878-1978* (Aldridge, n.d.)

Lichfield District Local Plan (Lichfield, 1994)

Lichfield Joint Record Office, Newscuttings Files

The Lichfield Mercury (1877-78)

Parker, Alfred, *A Sentimental Journey in and about the Ancient and Loyal City of Lichfield* (Lichfield, 1925)

Index

Abnalls, 76, 111, 115

Addison, Joseph, 71, 78, 79

Addison, Lancelot (dean) (1632-1703), 78

aerodrome, Fradley, 157, 159

air raids, 157

Alcock, John, 113, 114

alcohol, 94

Aldershawe, 23

Amphibalus, Christian priest, 3, 4

André, Major John, 103, 109

Anson, George, 138

army barracks, 145

army regiments, 143, 144

Arts Festival, 160

Ashmole, Elias, 70, 71-4, 77, 78

Ashmole, Thomas, 28

Ashmole family, 72

Aston, Elizabeth, 102

Aston Hall, Shrops., 13

asylums, 120-22

Bagot, Sir Edward, 69

Bagot, Richard, 61-2

Bakers Lane, 151, 161-2

Balaclava, Battle of, 145

Barber, Francis, 88

Barker, John, 134–5

barracks, Lichfield army, 145

Beacon Hill, 62

Beacon House, 156-7

Beacon Place, 150, 152

Beacon Street, 17, 21, 23, 30, 66-7, 79, 92, 112, 154

Beane, Hector, 24

Bellfounder, Henry, 23

Belmont School, Hassocks, 157

Bird Street, 5, 20, 92, 94, 96, 125, 128, 130-31, 160

Birmingham Road, 145

Bishops and Archbishops of Lichfield, 14-16, 18-22, 27, 39, 45, 49, 68, 70, 117

Bishop's Palace, 38, 62, 67, 70, 100-1, 121

Black Death, The, 39

Boley Park, 160

Boothby, Sir Brooke, 115, 162

Boothby, Penelope, 162

Bore Street, 20, 32, 94, 113, 122, 125-6, 148, 154

Borrowcop Hill, 4, 6, 9, 136, 153

Boswell, James, 83, 95, 97, 102

Boulton, Matthew, 104-5, 108, 110, 112

botany, 111

Bower Day, ix, 46-7, 140, 155

Bradley, Henry (philologist), 2

Breadmarket Street, 31, 72, 84, 89, 94, 122, 148

Brereton, Sir William, 62-6

brewing industry, 94, 128, 142, 149

Bridgeman, Robert, 39, 86, 165

Brindley, James, 111, 133-4

Brooke, Lord (Robert Greville), 53-5, 76

Brown, Trooper John, 145

Browne, Isaac Hawkins, 71

Buckeridge, Theophilus, 42

burgage plots, 20, 25

Burntwood, 23

Burton: Mary, 71; Walter, 71

Burton Road, 137

bus services, 141

Butler, James, 95

Camden, William, 3
canals, 133-7
Cannock, 18, 24, 58
Cannock Forest, 2
castle, 33
cathedral choir, 34-5, 113-14
cathedral close, 37-8, 53, 56, 60, 61, 65, 67, 99, 107, 115
Cathedral, St Chad's, 7, 11, 28, 32, 38-41, 44, 64-5, 68, 85, 127; bells, 70; statues, 39
Cathedral, St Chad's (Birmingham), 13
cattle markets, 150
Ceawlin, 7
Cecilian Society, The, 93
Cedd, 7
census 1695, 78
Chadwick, George (physician), 120-1
Chambers, Kitty, 88
Chantrey, Sir Francis, 152, 162
Chantries Act (1547), 43
chapel, Roman Catholic, 148
charities, 120
Charles II, King, 62
Charrington's shop, 82
Chesterfield, Earl of, 53, 56
Church Street, 150
cinemas, 156-7
Civic Hall, 156
Clinton, Roger de (bishop), 19-21
cloth trade, 27-8, 52
coachmakers, 95-6, 103, 110
Cobblers (Guild of Corvisers), 28
Cock Alley, 20
Coke, Thomas, 29
Colstubbe, 21, 76
Conduit Clock, 131-2
Conduit Lands Trust, 24-5, 70, 76, 92, 98, 120, 123-4, 126-8, 130-1, 153
Conduit Street, 24, 98, 125
Cooper, Sir Richard, M.P., 152, 165
Corn Exchange, 123
Corporation, Lichfield, 123-4, 127-8, 130-1

Corvisers, Guild of (Cobblers), 28
Couldery, Thomas, 124
court of array, ix, 163
Coventry cathedral, 15, 19, 42
Creton, Jean, 30
crime and punishment, 32, 49-50, 118, 125-6, 154, 158

Dam Street, 17-18, 37, 54-5, 64, 76, 85, 125
Darwin, Erasmus, 38, 77, 87, 94, 99, 102, 104, 109, 110-12, 133, 134-5, 140, 146
Davies, Private W.R., 143
Day, Thomas, 105-7, 109, 115
Deanery, 38
Defoe, Daniel, 39, 101
Diocletian (Pagan Emperor), 3
Doctor Milley's Hospital, 23
Domesday Book, 15, 17
Donegal House, 122
Drayton, John, 3
Dudley, Arthur, 12
Dugdale, William, 57, 77, 92
Dyot, Sir Richard, 53-4
Dyott family, 138

East, Michael (master of choristers), 72
Eccleshall Castle, 70
Eden, Sir Francis Morton, 118
Edial Hall, 80, 90
Edgeworth, Richard Lovell, 99, 101, 103-5, 107, 112
education, 34-6, 71, 118, 146, 153-4
Edward VI, King, 43
Egeraat, Erick van, 161
electricity, 125
Elizabeth I, Queen, 47
Elmhurst, 5
English Civil War, 52-66
Ethelbert, King, of East Anglia, 14
evacuees, 157

fairs, 25, 47
Farquhar, George, 79-80, 92

festivals and customs, ix, 45, 46-7, 113
Fiennes, Celia, 46, 68, 90
Finney, William, 120
Fitzherbert family, Swynnerton Hall, 13
Floyer, Sir John (physician), 76, 85, 91, 111
food and drink, 94
Ford, Sarah, 84
Fowlewell, 23
Fox, George, 48
Fradley aerodrome, 157, 159
Franklin, Benjamin, 112-13
French prisoners of war, 146
Frewen, Accepted (bishop), 69
Friary, The, 23, 41-2, 45, 131-2, 152
Friendly Societies, 119
Frog Lane, 20, 153, 162

Gage, Robert, 134
Gaia, 150
Gaia Lane, 17, 64
Gallows Wharf, 136
Garbett, Samuel, 134
Garrick, David, 71, 79-82, 85, 88, 101
Gas Company, Lichfield, 125
gas lighting, 125
Gastrell, Francis, Rev., 101-2
Gastrell, Jane, 102
Gell, Sir John, 55-6
Giffard family, 49
GKN, 159
Gough Square, 88
Graham-White, Claude, 143
Grammar School, 35, 71, 77-8, 101, 153
Greene, Richard, 74-6, 87, 137-8, 150
Greenhill Bower, ix, 117
Greenhill market, 25
Greville, Robert, 53-5, 76
Guildhall, x, 5, 32, 37, 43, 47, 48, 113, 115, 122-3, 125-6
Guild of St Mary and St John the Baptist, 31, 43

Hacket, John (bishop), 66, 68-9

Harris, Joseph, 39
Hartwell, John, 95
Hastings, Henry (Col.), 55-6
Hayley, William, 109
Hector, George, 85
Henry II, King, 18
Henry VIII, King, 11
Herckenrode, Belgium, 32
Herdman, W.G., 127
Heywood, Thomas (dean), 34, 38, 41
Heyworth, Bishop, 23
Hinkley family, 150
Hollcroft, William, 47
hospitals, 21-3, 35, 119, 156
housing, 160
Howard, John, 125
Howard, Mary, 109
Huddlesford, 136
Hull, Richard del (brother of St John's Hospital Chapel), 23
Hunter, John, 35, 77, 101
Hygeberht, Archbishop of Lichfield, 14

Improvement Commissioners, 124-5
industrial estate, 159
inns and public houses, 30, 42, 51, 92, 93
Irish in Lichfield, 148
Iron-Age Lichfield, 1

James II, King, 85
Johnson, Michael, 76, 84-5, 87, 97
Johnson, Samuel, 71, 76, 79-80, 83-6, 88-9, 98, 102
Johnson, Thomas (architect), 139

Kettle, Tilly, 100
Kilian, James A. (Col.), 158
King, Gregory, 77-8, 94

landmine, 59
Langton, Bishop, 11, 26, 27, 33, 117
Lastingham, Yorks., 7
Law, Thomas James, 130, 132, 165

Lectocetum/Letocetum: Roman name for Lichfield, 2
Leland, John (historian), 3, 10, 33-4
Leveson: Catherine, 69; Sir Richard, 69
Levetts Square, 161-2
Lewes, Joyce, 49
library, public, 130
Lichfield Aerated Water Co., 142
Lichfield and Hatherton Canal Restoration Trust, 137
Lichfield Botanical Society, 115
'Lichfieldensis' see Whittinton, Robert
Lichfield Gas Company, 125
'Lichfield kersey', 28
Lichfield Martyrs, 3-5
Lichfield Mercury, 25, 84, 143
Lichfield Races, 113
Lichfield Savings Bank, 123
Lichfield Working Men's Association, 154
Lido, The (cinema), 156-7
Lillingstone, Luke (Col.), 143-4
Linnaeus, 111
local government, 124, 127-8, 130, 163-4
London-Manchester air race, 143
Lombard Street, 17, 21, 95, 128, 137
Lucas, Richard Cockle, 83
Lunar Society, 104-5, 107, 112
lunatic asylums, 120-2
Lyccidfelth – placename, 2

McLean, John Robinson, 129, 140
market cross, 36-7, 47, 67
market gardens, 139, 149, 150
Market House, 98
markets and market square, 21, 25, 36-7, 47, 98, 123, 127, 141, 149-50, 165
Market Street, 20, 28, 56, 74, 97
Martyrs, Lichfield, 3-5
mental health, 120-2
Mercia, Kingdom of, 8, 13-14
Mesolithic, 1
metal industry, 29, 96
Methodist Hall, 157

militia, 144
Miller, James, 115
Milley, Thomas, 45; see also Doctor Milley's Hospital
mills, water, 17-18, 96, 130
Minster Pool, 18, 27, 32, 37, 65, 87, 129-30, 133-4
Moffat & Scott, 119
Monmouth, Geoffrey of, 3
monuments, 150-2, 156
Morgan, Major, 97
Moritz, Carl Philip, 96
Moseley, Cllr. Thomas (mayor), 158
museums, 74-6, 85, 126, 156
music, 113-14

Napper, Dennis, 51
Neile, Richard (bishop), 49-50
Nennius, 2
Neolithic, 1
Newboult, Samuel, 51
Newton, Andrew, 24
Newton's College, 24
Northumbria, 8
Norton Canes, 24
Nowell, Laurence, 44

Offa, King of Mercia, 14
Ogilby, John, 90
Oliver, Ann, 85-6
omnibuses, 138, 141

Paris, Matthew, 3
Parker, John, 52
parks and gardens, 130
parliamentary representation, 163
Pattingham church, 7
Paulhan, Louis, 143
Peada of Mercia, 8
Pearson, William, 63
Peel, Robert, 137
placenames, origins of, 1-3
plague, 51, 62-3

Plot, Robert, 5, 74, 90
police, 125-6
poll tax 1377, 30
poor relief, 117-20
population, 30, 51, 78, 128, 157, 160, 163, 165
Porter, Joseph, 102
Porter, Lucy, 88
postal system, 91
poverty, 117-20
Priests' Hall, 31
Prince Rupert's Mound, 59, 65, 150
prisoners of war, 146
probate inventories, 51
prostitution, 29-30
public art, 130
public baths, 76
public health, 125, 129
public houses and inns, 30, 42, 51, 89, 92-4, 140, 143
public library, 130

Quoniams Lane, 20, 85, 86, 125, 153

racing, 113
railways, 6, 131, 137-42, 160
railway stations: St John Street, 139-40; Streethay, 137, 139
Ramridge, John, 44
Rawson, James (physician), 10, 129
Ready, Thomas (Mayor of Lichfield), 138
redevelopment, 152, 157-9, 161-2
Reformation, The, 11, 41
Regal, The (cinema), 156
regiments, 143-4
Reynolds, Joshua, 89
Richard I, King, 18
Richard II, King, 30-1
Rixam, James, 92
Robinson, Ellen Jane, 152
Robinson, James, 122
Robinson, Marianne, 152
Robinson, William, 151

Romans in Lichfield, 1-2, 6
Roman roads, 1, 21, 137
Roundabout House, 98
Rous, John, 3
Rousseau, Jean Jacques, 105
Rowley Ragstone, 97
Rowley, Dr. Thomas, 121-22
Royal Air Force, 157
royal visits, 30, 47, 62
Rugeley, 18
Rupert, Prince, 58
Russel, Colonel, 58, 60
Ryknild Street, 1

Sadler Street, 84
St Chad, 4, 6-13, 41, 76
St Chad's Bath, 76
St Chad's cathedral, 7, 11, 28, 32, 38-41, 44, 64-5, 68-9, 85, 127; bells, 70; statues, 39
St Chad's cathedral, Birmingham, 13
St Chad's Gospels, 14
St Chad's Well, 10, 15
St James's Hall, 144, 154
St John's Hospital, 21-3, 35, 92
St John Street, 20-1, 27, 36, 70-1, 92, 94, 96, 120, 136, 139, 142, 148, 153
St John's Wharf, 136
St Mary's church, 11, 25, 33-4, 44, 67, 88, 126-7, 131
St Michael's church, 1, 5, 44, 76, 87-8, 119, 144-5, 146, 156
St Michael's Hospital, 119
St Peter's church, 11
Sandfield House (madhouse), 121
Sandfields Pumping Station, 129-30
Sandford Street, 95, 118-19, 125, 128, 148, 157
Saunders, Laurence, 44
Saville, John, 87, 107, 109, 111, 114-15
schools, 36, 71, 80, 85-6, 153-4
School of Art, 154
Scott, George Gilbert, 66, 119
Scott, Kathleen, 148

Scott, Sir Walter, 57-8, 109
Selwyn, George Augustus (bishop), 70
Seward, Anna, 47, 57-8, 87, 97, 99-101, 104, 107, 109, 115, 117, 145, 146, 148
Seward, Thomas, Rev., 100-1
Shaw, Robert, 78
Shaw, Stebbing, 46, 55, 75, 87, 88, 155
Shaw, William, 85
'Sheriff's Ride', 164
shopping centre, 161-2
Sidney, Sabrina, 106-7
Smalldridge, Anne, 52
Smirke, Samuel, 66
Smith, Cowperthwaite, 153
Smith, Francis, of Warwick, 122
Smith, Capt. Edward John, 130, 148
Snape, John, 87, 92, 149, 180
Sneyd, Elizabeth, 106-7, 109
Sneyd, Honora, 41, 102-3, 107, 109
societies, 93, 104, 119
South Staffordshire Junction Railway, 4, 138-9, 141
South Staffordshire Regiment, 143
South Staffordshire Waterworks Co., 129-30, 150
Stafford church, 7
Staffordshire Militia, 144
Staffordshire Yeomanry, 144-5
stage coaches, 92-3
statues, 39, 83, 130-1, 145
Stone, Sir Benjamin, 163
Stonyng, Gregory, 42-3
Stonynge, Julian, 51
Stotesbury, Lisle, 51
Stowe, 9
Stowe House, 102, 106, 150, 157
'Stowe Moggs' marshland, 87, 95
Stowe Pool, 17-18, 21, 37, 60, 61, 85-7, 95, 115, 129-30, 134
Stowe Street, 17, 88, 119
street cleansing, 125
street lighting, 124-5
streets and roads, 28, 91-2, 149, 160

'Swan Moggs', 87, 130
Swinfen, Dr. Samuel, 85, 91
Swynnerton Hall, 13; see also Fitzherbert

Tamworth Street, 20-1, 92, 94, 128, 156-7
theatres, 115-16, 154
Three Spires Shopping Centre, 162
tourism, 140, 162-3
trade and industry, 27-9, 51-2, 87, 94-6, 134, 136, 139, 141-2, 150, 158-62
Tradescant, John, 74
transport, 92-3, 95-6, 103, 133-43, 160
Trent, river, 2
Trent Valley Brewery Co., 142, 149
Trent Valley House, 158
Trent Valley Railway Company, 137-8
Trent Valley station, 130, 140, 142, 143
Trent Valley Trading Estate, 142
Tunstall, John, 95
turnpikes, 91-2, 135-6

Upper Pool, 37

Valor Ecclesiasticus, 42
Vicars, John, 57
Vikings in Lichfield, 14

Wade Street, 20, 156-7, 162
Walker, Richard (dean), 43
Wall, placename, 1-2, 6
Walmesley, Gilbert, 91, 101
watch, watchmen, 126
water mills, 17-18, 87, 130
water supply, 128-30
Waterworks Company, South Staffordshire, 129-30
Watling Street, 1
Wedgwood, Josiah, 112, 134-5
Wellington bombers, 157
Welsh links, 2, 6
Whittington Barracks, 113, 145, 157
Whittinton, Robert, 36, 41
Wightman, Edward, 50

William of Malmesbury, 19-20
William of St Albans (chronicler), 3
William the Conqueror, 17
Wilson, Benjamin, 80
Wissage Lane, 154
Women's Cheaping, 37
Wood, Thomas (bishop), 70
workhouses, 117-20
World War I, 156
World War II, 156-8
Wright, Joseph, of Derby, 110, 115

Wyatt, James, 124
Wyatt, John, 71
Wychnor, 134-5
Wychnor, Hugh of, 22
Wychnor Ironworks, 135
Wyrley and Essington Canal, 28, 136-7, 142

Yeomanry House, 153
Young, William, 2
Yoxall bridge, 91

81 A Plan of the City and Close of Lichfield from Actual Survey by John Snape, 1781.

A PLAN
of the
CITY and CLOSE
of
LICHFIELD,
from Actual Survey
By
JOHN SNAPE
81

A Century
SERMONS

Pinfold

Toll-gate

S T O W

M O G G S

Swan Moggs

MINSTER POO

SANDFORD

Workhouse

SANDFORD STREET

SADLER STREET

BOAR STREET

M A

Sandford Brook

Turks

Bowling Green

FRIERY

P A

P A R T O F S M A E L

School house Lane

Road from Birmingham

Engraved
BY
P. BEGBIE

The names of the War
Houses and Inhabitants

Bacon street Ward
Bird street Ward
Sandford street Ward
Sandford street below the W
St John street Ward
St John street above the Ba
Sadler street Ward
Boar street Ward
Wade street Ward
Dam street and Butcher ro
Tamworth street Ward
Lombard street Ward
Stow street Ward
Green hill Ward
Total within
Close

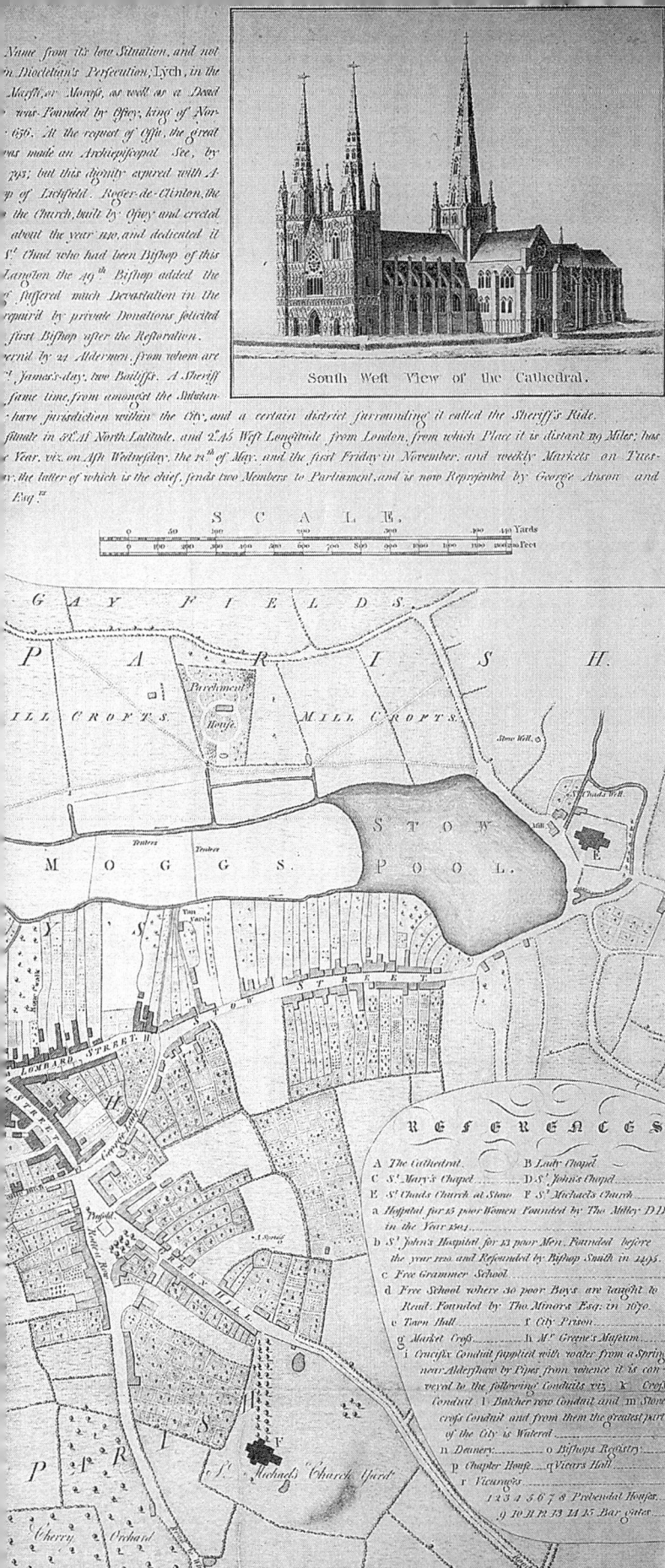

South West View of the Cathedral.

Name from its low Situation, and not
in Dioclatian's Persecution, Lych, in the
Maesh, or Morass, as well as a Dead
...were Founded by Oswy, king of Nor-
...656. At the request of Offa, the great
...was made an Archiepiscopal See, by
...793; but this dignity expired with A-
...hop of Lichfield. Roger-de-Clinton, the
...the Church, built by Oswy and erected
...about the year 1110, and dedicated it
...St. Chad who had been Bishop of this
...Langton the 49th Bishop added the
...suffered much Devastation in the
...repaird by private Donations solicited
...first Bishop after the Restoration.
...verned by 24 Aldermen, from whom are
...James's-day, two Bailiffs. A Sheriff
...same time, from amongst the Substan-
...have jurisdiction within the City, and a certain district surrounding it called the Sheriff's Ride.
...situate in 58° 41' North Latitude. and 2° 45' West Longitude from London, from which Place it is distant 119 Miles; has
...Year, viz. on Ash Wednesday, the 14th of May, and the first Friday in November, and weekly Markets on Tues-
...ay, the latter of which is the chief, sends two Members to Parliament, and is now Represented by George Anson and
...Esq.

S C A L E.

G A Y   F I E L D S.

P A R I S H.

Parchment
House

ILL CROFTS.   MILL CROFTS.   Stone Well.

St. Chads Well.

S T O W   P O O L.

Tenters   Tenter

M O G G S.

Tan Yards.

STREET

LOMBARD STREET.

REFERENCES

A The Cathedral.   B Lady Chapel.
C St. Mary's Chapel.   D St. John's Chapel.
E St. Chads Church at Stow F St. Michael's Church.
a Hospital for 15 poor Women Founded by Tho. Milley D.D.
    in the Year 1504.
b St. John's Hospital for 13 poor Men, Founded before
    the year 1100, and Refounded by Bishop Smith in 1495.
c Free Grammer School.
d Free School where 30 poor Boys are taught to
    Read, Founded by Tho. Minors Esq. in 1670.
e Town Hall.   f City Prison.
g Market Cross.   h Mr. Greene's Museum.
i Crucifix Conduit supplied with water from a Spring
    near Aldershaw by Pipes from whence it is con-
    veyd to the following Conduits viz. k Cross
    Conduit l Butcher row conduit and m Stow
    cross Conduit and from them the greatest part
    of the City is Watered.
n Deanery.   o Bishops Registry.
p Chapter House.   q Vicars Hall.
r Vicarage.
    1 2 3 4 5 6 7 8 Prebendal Houses.
    9 10 11 12 13 14 15 Bar gates.

St. Michaels Church Yard

P A R I S

Cherry   Orchard